Re-Arranging Your Mental Furniture

Changing Your Future for the Better

Ken Gaub

Treasure House

An Imprint of
Destiny Image® Publishers, Inc.
P.O. Box 310
Shippensburg, PA 17257-0310

"For where you treasure is, there will your heart be also."
Matthew 6:21

ISBN 0-7684-3028-3

(Previously published under ISBN 1-57502-480-2
by Morris Publishing.)

For Worldwide Distribution
Printed in the U.S.A.

This book and all other Destiny Image, Revival Press,
MercyPlace, Fresh Bread, and Treasure House books
are available at Christian bookstores and distributors worldwide.

For a U.S. bookstore nearest you, call **1-800-722-6774**.
For more information on foreign distributors, call **717-532-3040**.
Or reach us on the Internet: **http://www.reapernet.com**

Dedication

My parents, John and Millie Gaub, whose encouragement, daily (sometimes hourly) prayers, support, and faith helped me to keep on going.

My daughter Becki, who was persuaded at the last minute to help me finish this book.

All my friends and supporters...who believe in this ministry and continue to pray and support us so we can touch the world for God. How we thank God for the harvest. The best days are just ahead.

Special thanks to pastors of the greatest churches in the world, who bring me in to minister to their congregations. I love you all.

And finally, special thanks to Billy Joe Daugherty for allowing me to use his "Ten Commandments for Parents."

Quotes and Illustrations

Endorsements

Ken Gaub is one of the most inspiring persons I know. His ministry is always impactive, and he is ever on the alert to personally lead people to Christ. Many lives are always touched for God. The last time he was at Cypress Cathedral, I had our marquee along the highway read:

KEN GAUB

INSPIRATIONAL

MOTIVATIONAL

INDESCRIBABLE

Rev. Dwight Edwards
Cypress Cathedral
Winter Haven, Florida

God has given Ken Gaub the ability to present powerful truths and principles with humor and a motivational punch. I've often wondered what vantage point he has that enables him to see things so uniquely. When you look through Ken's eyes, you feel as if you're seeing things for the first time.

Willard Thiessen
"It's a New Day"
Trinity Television, Inc.
Winnipeg, Manitoba, Canada

Ken Gaub is a great communicator. He finds where you are, then leads you on a journey that involves laughter, instruction, inspiration, and God's principles. When you hear Ken, you are motivated to be all that God intends you to be. We love him here at First Assembly.

Rev. Alton Garrison
First Assembly of God
North Little Rock, Arkansas

Ken Gaub is a true minister. His ability to teach using the medium of humor is delightful. His walk with God has been a remarkable journey that will inspire faith in all who hear him or read his books.

Rev. Leroy Lebeck
Trinity Church
Sacramento, California

If there is one word that describes Ken Gaub, it is *unique*. Ken is an author, gifted speaker, Bible teacher, evangelist, motivator, comedian, husband, grandfather, Christian, and loyal friend. Ken is also a man on a mission with infectious enthusiasm. If you are not inspired after personal exposure to Ken Gaub, then you are also unique.

Rev. John Lloyd
Countryside Christian Center
Clearwater, Florida

Ken Gaub is a creative soul winner, one who motivates others to do the same. Always behind his excitement and fun is a desire to help hurting people. He has a unique goal of keeping his scheduled appearances. Once he drove all night over snowbound roads when his airline flight was canceled because of weather and everyone else was stranded. Several hours and two hundred miles later he was on time to speak at our church. He considered his appearance there of highest priority and an emergency as an ambassador of Heaven's government.

Rev. James Menke
New Hope Christian Center
Lima, Ohio

Once again, Ken hits the nail on the head with this book. Attitude is everything! He communicates this dynamic principle in his inimitable style and then lays out a clear path to a better tomorrow for you. Ken Gaub is a motivator, visionary, leader, and my friend. He practices what he preaches at home as well as on the road. As a fellow motivator, visionary, and pastor, that impresses me. Give this book a read. It will change your life!

Pastor Jon Oletzke
Stone Church
Yakima, Washington

Ken Gaub is a very rare combination of preacher, motivator, author, father, husband, and friend. His books reflect his sensitivity in all areas of life. Ken's writing will keep you reading and growing. The humor in Ken's messages makes spiritually palatable some rather heavy thoughts. These would be a load to carry if it were not for his unique ability to give a bit of jest that does no damage to the principle but enables it to be extremely effective.

Don Lyon, D.D.
Faith Center
Rockford, Illinois

Contents

Foreword

Ken Gaub...is a soul winner.

Ken's heart is set on knowing God and helping others also know Him. He is just as interesting in person as when he is speaking to thousands. He wants people to know Christ as Savior in their lives. Ken's ministry at Victory Christian Center in Tulsa has always been outstanding. Not only do the lost find Christ during his meetings, but Christians also are inspired to win others outside the church as they go about their daily lives.

Rev. Billy Joe Daugherty
Victory Christian Center
Tulsa, Oklahoma

Introduction

Never—even in my wildest dreams—was it ever my goal to write books. I always thought *authors* wrote books. Then early one morning I asked myself, *"What is the main reason I am doing another book?"*

Is it because I now know everything? Trust me, that certainly is not the answer.

Is it because I never get angry or have a bad attitude and always treat everyone right all the time? That isn't right either.

Maybe after all these years I now know how to succeed without failing, so it's time to share? That's also a long way from the truth.

Maybe since I always practice what I preach, I can tell others how to do it? I wish that were so. Sometimes I feel guilty when negatives hit my life. I have feelings, I can be hurt, and believe it or not, I'm also human.

It's probably due to the fact that everyone loves me and I have no enemies. I'm sure that I have my share. It's impossible to please everyone all the time.

My friend...*the real reason* behind authoring another book is twofold.

1. God wanted you to hear it.
2. I love helping others find answers to life's problems.

While I was writing, I remembered the many letters I have received from all over the world from people who talked about my other books or from those who saw me in person in their area or heard a tape or watched a video. All the effort is worth it, when people are helped!

Of course, this new book may not be perfect in every way. Some people read books to look for mistakes or contradictions. I am simply teaching what has helped me. My soul burned as I wrote the following pages. Many struggle to get through a day; others struggle in their job, in their marriage, or innumerable other ways.

I'm committed to a lifetime of helping people who need answers in their lives. I may step on your toes, but it's not to mess up the shine on your shoes. As you read, you will understand why I think like I do, and I trust you will take steps to turn things around. You can, because with God's help *all things are possible!*

One of the greatest positive thinkers of all time was poor—a Jew, with few of what we call opportunities. He came from the wrong area of the country. He had to work as a simple laborer, gained little of the world's goods, and died broke. He never traveled more than a few miles from home. He was not well connected—had none of what we call "friends in high places." His companions were the sick, the needy, the working class, crooked politicians, and tax collectors. He succeeded in His mission by dying, but that death completely changed the world.

Introduction

His name was Jesus, and He was and is the Son of God. Jesus can set us free.

My prayer is that:

You will find God's perfect will for your life.
You will change your attitude for the better.
You will face all challenges with a determined faith in God.
You will learn to take the opportunities that God places before you.
You will make stepping-stones out of your failures.
You will have a wonderful home and family.
You will make decisions that really count.
You will have health and healing.
You will be blessed financially, prospering beyond your wildest dreams.
You will have a honeymoon marriage (if you are married).
*You will believe in the **Jesus factor**.*

Now...let's get your hopes up for a great future. You can have that unbeatable thinking. You can have a correct image of who God really is and what He wants to do for you. Your tomorrows will be better than your yesterdays.

This is my prayer.

There are two sure things in life: 1) There is a God! 2) You are not Him (and neither am I).

Ken Gaub

Chapter One

How We Think—And Why

When the full force of "thinking right" hit me, it went deep into my heart. I began to realize that I didn't think right about a lot of things, and I became determined to change. You can too.

In this book we're going to deal with a lot of things concerning our thinking. Wrong thinking does not produce right results. Negative thinking will never produce positive results.

Many things can cause us to form good or bad thoughts: our past, our knowledge of God's Word, how we feel about ourselves, and our general physical and emotional health. Even our dreams and goals affect our thinking.

This might sound like New Age thinking, but it's not. New Age thinking is not an organized, consistent, or cohesive set of teachings. It is a conglomeration of ideas borrowed from many diverse religions and philosophies, and it is *not* Christian. One or another New Ager might use or claim to use some solid

1

Christian teachings, but they twist and push those Christian teachings out of balance to fit them under the New Age umbrella. New Age thinking focuses on one's self (not the biblical God) as supreme, and it goes downhill from there. Obviously, I'm against New Age teaching.

Few people think more than once or twice a year. I have made an international reputation by thinking once or twice a week.

George Bernard Shaw

What Your Thoughts Do

Your thinking can help make you into a success or a failure. Your thinking will help you overcome or cause you to struggle. Your thoughts can make you free, or they can put you in prison. They can help you or hurt you. They can lift you up or tear you down. They can make you love or hate, laugh or cry, advance or retreat. They can make you a winner or a whiner. Your thoughts control the way you react to situations. Your life can grow or shrink, thrive or fail. It all depends on how you think about it.

We can change negative thinking to positive thinking and negative actions to positive actions. When we begin to think differently, we function differently, and, in turn, our future will change. To help you picture the process, let's view shifting our thought patterns as rearranging our mental furniture. Now, thinking positively—thinking right—doesn't mean you're a New Ager. There are many positive-thinking ministers to whom we could listen in order to change our thinking and our future. The Bible tells us in Proverbs 23:7 that as a man "thinketh in his heart, so is he"—the words of Solomon, a wise man.

How We Think—And Why

A small boy was sitting beside the road with a puppy and a sign stating, "DOG FOR SALE. 25 CENTS." A businessman on his way to work stopped to talk to the boy.

"Son," he said, "that's a mighty fine dog. You need to raise your price." That night on his way home, he noticed that the sign now read, "DOG FOR SALE. $5,000." He smiled.

The next morning the sign was down but the boy was there, so the man stopped to talk to him again. "Did you really sell the dog for $5,000?" he asked.

"Well, not exactly," admitted the child, "but I traded him for two $2,500 cats!"

I guess it's all in how you look at things.

It has been stated many times that life is 10 percent what happens to us and 90 percent how we react to what happens to us.

You can get bogged down in frustrations and get discouraged or run into seemingly impossible situations and be defeated, or you can walk tall, whistle, and laugh rather than whimper and whine. Close the doors of your thought life to fear, envy, anger, and bad attitudes. Open the doors of your thought life to miracles, answers, faith in God, power from the Holy Spirit, and positive possibilities. God can help you think about the good things He is going to do for you. If you want God to give you miracles, then you have to prepare to receive those miracles.

Yes, I know there is more to it than just thinking. Unless we act upon our thoughts, they remain just thoughts. The message of Jesus was a positive one. He taught action, not passivity—active trust, not passive surrender. He is our ultimate example.

I've often wondered why some people succeed when they are less talented than others. The answer is that they have learned to overcome, to look at situations in a totally different manner. They've faced unbelievable tragedy with faith in a God who will see them through. They are enthusiastic and optimistic. They have confidence. They have faith. They break records, and they make things work. Thank God for this kind of people.

I believe the greatest miracles have yet to be accomplished, and it is this kind of people who will be there when they do. I have heard ministers say that they could never build a great church with thousands attending, but I believe that the greatest churches in the world have yet to be built. And why not? Take Tommy Barnett, a friend of mine. I assure you that he is a mortal, but he works with God in building a church that touches the world and that will continue to grow. The lives of visionary men like Tommy should challenge others to do more. Believe me, God has no exclusive contract with Tommy.

Tommy's son, Matthew, is pastoring a church in the inner city of Los Angeles, which is making a difference in lives both now and for eternity. When I was there to speak, I was amazed at what is happening. What a ministry! But believe me, God has no exclusive contract with either Tommy or Matthew. You can also touch your world for God.

Renew Every Morning

Every morning a wonderful thing happens to me. It makes no difference where I am in the world. It happens every day: I wake up breathing. That's exciting when you think about it! When I wake up, I think about what a great day it will be. I pray and tell the Lord of my love for Him, that I'm going to serve Him and obey Him. I say, "God, whatever You're doing today, I want to be a part of it. I'm not asking You just to bless what I do. Please let me do what You are blessing. Fill my

4

thoughts and my mind with good, positive things for today. I may face many challenges, but I know You'll see me through." I want God to be proud of me. (See Job 13:15.)

The greatest moments in our lives lie just ahead. I look for them. I think about them. I get excited about them. I'm going to receive them. If you want God to give you miracles, you have to prepare to receive those miracles. When you get up in the morning, praise God for another day. Refuse to let yesterday or past problems enter your mind. "Submit yourselves therefore to God. Resist the devil, and he will flee from you" (Jas. 4:7). Take your stand at the beginning of the day. Get into partnership with God as soon as you wake up.

It's important how we think. I can't stress that enough. Each person's mind is a billion-dollar gift from God. No computer can match its capabilities. We seldom tap into even a small portion of its potential. Romans 8:5-6 (NKJV) says, "For those who live according to the flesh set their minds on the things of the flesh, but those who live according to the Spirit, the things of the Spirit. For to be carnally minded is death, but to be spiritually minded is life and peace." God made our minds for a purpose.

Our minds cannot be physically touched or seen. They are like computer programs written on our brains. Just like a computer, we make decisions and draw conclusions from the material we feed into our minds. But unlike a computer, our minds can draw more than just one set of conclusions from each situation.

Who Are We?

How we think can even determine how we will feel. We live in a world that is so phony and full of pretense that we need to think about who we really are. The way we carry ourselves, the

5

way we walk, the way we talk, and even the way we dress all reflect the way we actually think. That's why I say that a personal relationship with God affects all aspects of our lives.

Doug Graves, a pastor friend of mine, has written a book titled, *Who Do You Think You Are?* He states, and I quote:

"A Christian mind that has not been renewed to the truth of his new identity in Christ will be robbed of the abundant life God has provided for him. God wants you to have a deeper understanding of what He has made you in Christ.

"How you see yourself definitely determines how your life will be lived out. Someone said, 'You cannot consistently live in a way that is inconsistent with the way you see yourself.' You can only live the God kind of life when true identity in Christ is rediscovered.

"You are an offspring of God. You are not children of God in an intellectual way. You are in reality children of the One who created all things...Jesus didn't die just to take away sins. Jesus came to undo what the first Adam did and restore man to his place of relationship with God. You were created in His image and His likeness. It is time to let your mind be renewed and discover the person that God has made you in Christ."[1]

You can't have a better tomorrow if you're thinking about yesterday all the time.
Charles F. Kettering

---

1.   Doug Graves, *Who Do You Think You Are?*, (Kennewick, WA: Word of Faith Center, 1999) 3-4,5,12-13.

6

How We Think—And Why

It's amazing how many of our crises and challenges could be solved if we'd just use common sense and think things through. Many times we try to do everything *but* think because thinking seems to be such a hard thing to do. You may say, *"It's my job, it's my family, it's my challenges that make me the way I am."* Too many of us blame others. Sometimes we even blame God. The real truth of the matter is that the way we think about those things and react to them makes us what we actually are.

I believe that it is often easier for God to do difficult things for us than easy things. We tend to feel that the easy things will work out anyway, whether or not we ask for God's help. But with the more difficult things, we give up, get out of God's way, and totally depend on Him.

Success doesn't just fall out of the sky onto your head. You do things that put you on the path to success. You will never change the way things are in your life until you change the way you think. Then you will change the way you do things, and as a result, your future changes.

You might still be asking, *"Ken, why is my thinking so important?"* One reason is that our thinking affects our total believing. Our believing, in turn, controls the way we talk and how we live. It becomes a cycle. We can get caught up in the wrong cycle. Faith in God will help us break negative cycles in our lives and tear down the strongholds of satan. Faith in God thus helps us develop the quality thinking that the Bible teaches. It's so refreshing, so exciting to think in a positive manner. So let's eliminate our negative thoughts and replace them with *positive* thoughts. No wonder Paul stated, "Whatsoever things are true...honest...just...pure...lovely...of good report; if there be any virtue, and...any praise, think on these things" (Phil. 4:8). God wants our minds to be filled with good things.

---

*C*hange *your thoughts, and you change your world.*

Norman Vincent Peale

When negative thoughts hit you, interrupt them and recall the good things God is blessing you with. Think about the good things. When a challenge hits your life, start thinking differently about that challenge. Don't take a negative approach, thinking about all the things that won't work. Start looking *for* the answer instead of *at* the problem. Look for things that could work. Look for as many possible solutions as you can. Refuse to let the problem wear your spirit down. God is always bigger than our challenges. Stop telling God how big the problem is and start telling your problem how big God is!

When your thinking is right, it can help you overcome all of life's limitations. Right thinking will change your world. It will help you jump over every obstacle. I firmly believe that our lives move in the direction of our most dominant thoughts. I think about winning people to Christ, so my life moves in that direction.

Suppose a man has planned a fishing trip, but the night before, all his fishing gear is stolen. Most avid fishermen will find some way to beg or borrow enough tackle to still go fishing. If something happens to a hunter's favorite gun, he will do whatever he needs to do so that he won't miss his hunting expedition.

If you are a sports fan and your television quits working, you will call a friend and go to his house to watch "the game" on his TV. On the way over, you will keep track of the score on the radio or by talking to the friend on your cell phone.

The importance of the fishing, hunting, or sports event will overshadow everything else. It is easy to see where the dominant thoughts lie.

As I said before, I think mostly about winning people to Christ, so my life moves in that direction. Wherever I am—airports, restaurants, hotels, taxis, airplanes—I meet people who are waiting to find Christ as Savior. I lead dozens of them to Him every year.

The negative thoughts that hit our lives are the worst bandits that we'll ever face.

Dan Wold

We make two errors. We overestimate the other fellow's brain power, and we underestimate our own. As a result, we fail to do things. Then along comes someone who doesn't worry about brain power, and he is able to see miracles happen.

More men fail through lack of purpose than through lack of talent.

Billy Sunday

Many things begin in our thought life. A person who watches pornography will end up thinking that it is normal. Rape, sexual violence, divorce, murder, robbery—all begin with thinking. The prophet in Isaiah 26:3 predicted, "Thou wilt keep him in perfect peace, whose mind is stayed on Thee: because he trusteth in Thee." We all think about wholesome things other than God. We think about our families, food, sleeping, traveling. But just thinking about wholesome things is not enough. Our minds need to be focused upon God.

Some people think about romance; others about material things. Some think about drugs and pornography, or about New

Age ideas. These individuals don't think about the things of God. Some people don't even know what they're thinking!

Are thoughts of financial problems and debt bombarding your mind? Don't give up; combat those thoughts with the promises of God. His desire is to prosper your life in a special way.

As Second Corinthians 10:4-5 states, "The weapons of our warfare are not carnal, but mighty through God to the pulling down of strong holds; casting down imaginations, and every high thing that exalteth itself against the knowledge of God, and bringing into captivity every thought to the obedience of Christ." Paul says that the greatest warfare is in our thought life. We need victory over the negative thoughts that control our life. Cultivate a relationship with God.

A woman told me she would be glad when she got to Heaven because there she would have victory over the devil. I replied that she needed victory here, not there, because the devil wouldn't be in Heaven.

Nothing in life changes for the better unless we choose to change. Most of us don't have to do anything special to become overweight. It takes effort to lose the extra pounds and keep them off. We have to choose to do it. It doesn't take much effort to have a messy house, but it takes determination and discipline to keep it neat. Our mind is the same way. It can become messy. Satan and the negative world around us will produce all kinds of things that will cause our minds to get messed up. It takes work to keep it clean and our thoughts positive.

Jesus said, "It is the thought life that defiles you" (Mk. 7:20 TLB). Our thoughts can be deadly to us. We all think or meditate every day. Meditation is merely thinking about something for a long period of time. When you control your mind, you control your thinking. In Colossians chapter 3, verses 1-5 and 9-10, we are told to set our minds on things above, not on the things of this earth. Set your thought life on the things of God. In Isaiah 55:7-9, God says that His thoughts are not our thoughts. We need to forsake our own thoughts and begin thinking like God wants us to think.

We must start thinking that we are going to be better parents. We need to be thinking about having better relationships with those around us—with our family, children, and friends. We need to be thinking about prospering financially and giving more to God's work. We need to focus on keeping the things around us orderly and neat. We *can* become excellent people and start thinking the way God wants us to.

Worldly Thinking

It's amazing how our country thinks. In today's world, we want instant solutions. We don't think things through as we look for quick answers. There are one-hour photo labs, one-hour dry cleaners, fast food drive-thru windows, and quick delivery for pizza. We want things to be instant, even in relationships, finances, and weight loss. We live in a microwave world. We want it done *now*. Not everything works like that.

Wrong habits, lustful ideas, envy, anger, strife, and jealousies can only bring harm to your mind. But you can't fix them quickly. Don't let your mind become the devil's playground. It is the entrance to your soul. If satan can get your mind, he's got your soul.

Satan is out to destroy us. Television conveys the impression that immorality and homosexuality are normal. The forces of the world do not condemn adultery and fornication.

Some people say:

1. *Why get married? We'll just live together. Others are doing it; it's okay.*

11

2. *Why have proper diet and exercise? That's too much work.*
3. *I don't know how to fix my finances. More credit must be the answer.*
4. *Children are such a pain; I'll have an abortion.*
5. *We don't need a relationship; we need sex now.*
6. *I don't need a job. If I can pull a few strings, I can live off the government.*
7. *Why clean the house? It'll just get messed up again. Why wash the car? It's going to rain.*

That type of thinking is what's gotten America into its present situation. We need a shift in our thinking.

We have gone so far in our loss of values. That's why in America, every day, thousands of unwed girls between 15 and 19 have babies. That's why kids take guns to school. That's why more than 50 million Americans are hooked on nicotine. That's why more than 15 million are alcoholics. That's why more than three million are on cocaine and more than two million on intravenous drugs.

Use your head for something besides a hat rack.

Jim Agard

I suggest that you write down your problems, then start thinking about them in a different manner. Shift your mental gears in God's direction.

If you plant an acorn in the ground, an oak tree will grow. If you plant peas, you'll harvest peas. If you plant strawberries, you'll get strawberries. As we sow, we reap. The same is true of our thinking. Bad actions come from bad thoughts. Good thoughts produce good actions, which then produce good results. It requires thinking right, however. Let's plant good seed in fertile ground.

Sometimes we need to stop worrying too far into the future. (Don't get this confused with setting long-term goals.) Jesus prayed, "Give us this day our daily bread" (Mt. 6:11). Learn how to live daily with your thought life. Think, *Today will be a great day. All fears and worries will be gone. God will see me through. I'm not going to worry about next year. Right now I just want to take care of today. I know God will help me.* Your thoughts will produce the energy you need. God wants you to start believing His Word and thinking that all things are possible with God. (Read Mark 9:22-23.)

Believe that God has miracles in the making for you. Start thinking in the way of believing. Quit thinking about the past, about the hurts, about those who have cheated you. Start living by faith and start thinking about what God can do. It will set your soul afire. It will do great things for you.

Quit being afraid of how others think and begin considering how God thinks. Hold on to the possibility of miracles. Shift your mental gears.

Small and Big Thinkers

The way we think is more important than how much intelligence we possess. Small thinkers say things differently from the way big thinkers do. When you think you can do something great, you usually do. When you don't think you can do it, you usually don't. Why? When you start thinking and saying that it's going to be a long, hard process, it usually goes that way.

Thinking big and believing God for big things is important in our lives. To be a successful thinker does not require a super intellect. The size of our thinking determines the size of our accomplishments. We need to enlarge our thinking. Think a little bigger; think a little greater. Think a little higher, a little nicer.

If you say something won't work and set out to prove that it won't work, you are thinking small. But if you say it will work and go out to prove that it will work, you have hope of something greater.

People say, *"Count me out; it won't happen."* Say instead, *"Count me in; it will happen."* If you say there's no use trying, you've already failed. Instead, just keep trying until you find a new way to make that thing work. It's all in how you think about it.

You sometimes have to look at what could be instead of what is right now. Ephesians 3:20 says that the Lord "is able to do exceeding abundantly above all that we ask or think." I can think pretty big, but God is greater than my ability to even imagine. I want Him as my partner.

We can choose to use our thinking in a positive way, or we can doubt and go on as we are.

Your emotions and actions are the belated announcement of what you have been thinking.
Dave Hess

You can't think poverty and have wealth. You can't think sickness and have health. You can't think failure and have success. Don't limit your thinking. (Read Psalm 78:1-11.)

Human behavior is amazing and puzzling. People who command the most respect are the most successful. Thinking helps make that happen. We receive the kind of treatment we think we deserve. If you think you're inferior and worthless, you may be making a self-fulfilling prophecy. If you think you're unimportant, you're probably right. If you think you are

14

important, are a special creation of God—a unique personality— and can achieve your dreams, then you are and you can.

To gain respect, you have to believe you deserve it. Look important, act important, talk important (but not arrogant). We need first-class thinking. Small-thinking people will hold you back from reaching your goals. It's been said that if we help make others successful, we will become successful also. Success can depend on the support of others. Our thinking about other people must be right.

Networking is a big buzzword in business today. The principle is that people work together, each one doing the things that he does best. Not everyone does all tasks with equal ease, but each uses his skill for the betterment of the others within the network. No one has jealousy toward another, but each helps and recommends the skill of the others both within and outside of the network. It becomes unnecessary to "reinvent the wheel" each time a new skill is needed.

Set your standards higher. Think that you will succeed and improve everything in your life. We've all heard it said, "*If every member were a member like me, what kind of church would this church be?*" Do you think positively about yourself? Your family? Your job or your business? We need to put these principles to work.

A person came to me who had been in a multi-level marketing business, but who was no longer involved. His former associates had completely cut him off and were telling lies about him because he had left. Needless to say, he was hurt and disappointed. I advised him to put it behind him and move on. Remember, it's not what happens to us that matters as much as how we react to what happens.

Take time to think about things. Think success, believe for success, have faith for success. Believe God will give you the success that He desires to give you.

Think differently about how to handle things. Shift your thought patterns—rearrange your mental furniture.

N*o person would go into the world half dressed; wise people consider themselves well dressed when their mind is wearing a positive idea as a shield against negative forces in the world.*

Dr. Robert Schuller

Paul states in Philippians 4:13 that we "can do all things through Christ which strengtheneth [us]." Sometimes we talk ourselves into being total failures by talking negatively. We moan, *"I can't make it. It's impossible. I'm fed up."* Our thinking is moving in the wrong direction. We need to tell ourselves, *"I can do all things. Things are going to change, with the Lord's help. The possibilities are tremendous. I'm looking for answers. I'm a problem solver. I believe God will see me through."*

The story is told of two salesmen who were sent to Africa to sell shoes. One wired back to the company: "Returning home. No one here wears shoes." The other wired: "Rush more shoes. Great potential for sales. No one has shoes."

Start saying every day:

> **Jesus is in my life. (Be sure that He is.)**
> **God has made me a unique creation.**
> **I'm looking forward to a great future.**
> **Days of opportunity are here now.**

16

Great things will happen.

I'm going to stay cheerful, even when I'm not happy.

I will control circumstances.

I will interrupt all negative thoughts.

I will be a giver.

I will obey God.

All my problems are simply opportunities.

I can do more than I think I can.

I'm enthusiastic about the future.

I have God-given energy.

I am a winner, not a whiner.

I will use challenges as stepping-stones.

God will help me to tap the necessary resources to succeed.

I'm sure we've all seen how positive-thinking people have reached goals and turned their dreams into reality. They've taken the problems they faced and turned them into victories. Their lives have been transformed. Jesus said that if we have faith as a grain of mustard seed, we can tell a tree to be cast into the sea and it would do it. (See Luke 17:6.) Nothing will be impossible to us. Let's build a relationship with God who is our only source of power and the One who gives us the ability to make things happen. Then we can have a shift in thinking and change to the way God wants us to think.

You need to take thirty minutes a day with paper and pen and Bible and just think. It can change your life.

Sam Smucker

Notes

Shift your thinking:

1. Do I have a personal relationship with God?

2. What areas in my thought life are based on the Word of God?

3 What areas in my thought life are carnally based?

4. What things do I think about that have produced negatives in my life?

5. What things do I think about that have produced positives in my life?

6. What things do I think about that hinder my future?

Top Three Changes to Make!

1.

2.

3.

Chapter Two

God's Will

God has a blueprint for your life and my life. He has a plan. His carefully laid-out plan for salvation is part of His overall plan for each one of us. It is not His will that anyone misses Heaven. It doesn't matter what has happened to us or where we are in our life, God has a plan for us. Your failure or success depends on letting God work out His plan, His will, in your life.

Sometimes God doesn't tell us His plan because we wouldn't believe it anyway.

Carlton Pearson

I don't believe that anything happens by chance with God. I believe God puts people into our lives for a reason. In fact, it is God's will that you are reading this book right now.

Do you know the direction that God has for your life? Do you know the plan that God has for you? Is the plan laid out?

Do you understand it? Do you understand why you need a plan? Have you talked to God about it?

Good Things

It is God's will that good things happen to you. Because God has a perfect plan for your life, it's His will that certain things happen.

Romans 8:28 states that "all things work together for good to them that love God." It does not say that everything is good, but that God can take everything, good or bad, that crosses our pathway and cause it to work to our advantage. *Does God allow suffering in the life of a Christian? Does He even arrange it? Read on.*

God will take the broken, messed-up pieces of a ruined, wasted life and use them to build a life that brings honor to His name. That is the ultimate in recycling.

Have you ever made the decision to go for God's perfect will, not just His permissive will? God will often permit us to have our own way, if we insist, even when He has a better way. Unlike many of us, God is a gentleman who will not impose His will upon us, even when He knows that we are wrong.

How do you know that you have made the right decisions about His will? Sometimes people chase things that turn out to be harmful to them because they don't go by biblical guidelines.

Start by searching the Bible, God's written Word. Certain things are specifically either commanded or forbidden. Other things are implied by principle. Seek godly advice. Write down all the pros and cons and study them prayerfully. Use your own mind, and put all that you discover into your own God-given "personal computer." But always remember that the urging of the Spirit will never contradict what's in the Bible.

Christians are not just the hunted, but the hunters; not the attacked, but the attackers. We are God's storm troopers.

Reinhard Bonnke

It's important that we know the difference between God's will and our will. Some things are God's will; some are our will. Our will should be surrendered to Him, so that His will becomes our will.

One of the big questions of all time is this: *Why do the godly suffer? Are times of trial God's will?* The apostle Peter discusses this in First Peter 1:6-7. His conclusion is "that the trial of [our] faith...might be found unto praise and honour." He goes on to tell us in First Peter 2:21 that Jesus left us an example by His suffering, and in First Peter 5:10 he asks God that we be made perfect, established, strengthened, and settled. Paul wrote that our "suffering produces perseverance; perseverance, character; and character, hope" (Rom. 5:3-4 NIV).

Israel has had more than its share of testing and suffering in the 50 or so years it has existed as a modern nation. There have been many heroes from among its people. One young man, a Jew born in Egypt, was sent by the Israeli intelligence service first to South America and then on to Syria to gather information about what military strikes might be planned against Israel.

He was able to establish himself as a Syrian businessman so successfully that he became friends with the top military and political leaders within the Syrian government. He was taken on a tour of an extremely sensitive area overlooking northern Israel, and he became responsible for planting shade trees around all the bunkers, supposedly to make the bunkers cooler for the Syrian soldiers. However, they also effectively marked the bunkers, making them easy targets for the Israelis.

During the Six Day War in 1967, because of those trees identifying the bunkers, Israel was able to take this heavily fortified area within just a few hours. Unfortunately, Eli Cohn had been caught and publicly executed two years previously. Nevertheless, his efforts had been instrumental in saving the nation of Israel from destruction at the hands of her enemies.

Was his death good? I think not. But did his efforts help accomplish God's purpose for Israel? History gives a resounding "YES."

God's Will for Jesus

Even Jesus had a moment, in the Garden of Gethsemane, when He had to surrender His will to that of the Father. (See Matthew 26:36-46.) As He looked ahead, He knew that the Father's will for Him was to take the sins of the world to the cross and to be a sacrifice for our redemption. But He also looked at it from the human standpoint. The pain, the agony, the suffering, the rejection, and the momentary separation from the Father made the prospect so painful that He actually sweat great drops of blood.

God's Will for You

You might feel the same way at times, torn between two decisions. In your spirit, you know what to do, but sometimes you make the wrong decision. Sometimes you choose something that is not God's will because the decision seems so painful. If we're going to fulfill the will of God, though, we have to walk in the Spirit so we don't fulfill the lusts of the flesh. (See Galatians 5:16.) We must understand that our relationship with God is of primary importance.

Some people have given up prospective mates who didn't fit into what they knew was God's will for their lives. A friend who had not married by the time she was 26 said, "I'm sure that it's God's will for me to be married, but there's nobody in sight!" I told her not to panic; God had a living, breathing man in existence for her.

She responded in humor, "Let him breathe on me." It was only a short time until she began dating a young man whom she married a few months later. They now have two beautiful children. Their marriage has been blessed—all because she refused to settle for a counterfeit of God's will for her life.

People can lose their business, home, and everything they possess because of their own will. It's important to surrender our will to Christ's. It is the will of God, not ours, that is important. As always, in this Jesus is our great example.

Is it God's will to be sick? I don't believe that it is. John said that he wished above all things that his friend would "prosper and be in health" (3 Jn. 2). It is God's will that we be blessed. Because we live in a sick and sinful world, negative things can come into our lives—sometimes because of stupid things that we have done that were our will, not His.

I believe that it is God's will to be healthy. It is a benefit that God has promised to us. A truly Christian lifestyle is a basically healthy lifestyle. Most of us refuse to pollute our bodies with drugs, alcohol, and tobacco, but how many of us use the same care in our eating habits? We seem to forget that we also can defile our bodies by overeating. We are admonished by Paul to treat our bodies with the same respect that we would treat the temple of God. (See First Corinthians 3:16.)

But if you are sick, get your eyes off of the sickness and start believing that God will turn things around for you. God wants us well. Jesus was so concerned about sickness that He took the stripes for our healing. (See Isaiah 53:5.) God promised that He is the Lord who heals. He promised to take sickness from the midst of us. (See Exodus 23:25.) Healing is of God. "He sent His word, and healed them" (Ps. 107:20a).

God doesn't want to keep His blessings from you. If you are not on the receiving end of blessings, stop blaming the devil, your spouse, your relatives and friends, or your circumstances. The real problem may be your own attitude about God's will for you.

What is the will of God in your life? We need to keep the desire for that uppermost in our thinking. It is God's will for you to be blessed in every way. You can expect it. You can count on it; you can figuratively "take it to the bank." If your relationship to God is right, it will flip your switch, float your boat, raise your flag, turn you on, and get you excited. If you have no relationship with God, or at the least one that is shallow, you'll bail out the first time the boat springs a leak.

You are today getting ready for a great future in the will of God.

Rick Thomas

Notes

1. Trust God's will for your life.

2. Believe that God wants good things to happen to you.

Top Three Changes to Make!

1.

2.

3.

Chapter Three

Attitudes for Success

Your attitude is a very important part of your life. Remember, 10 percent of life is what actually happens to you, and 90 percent is how you react to what happens. In our lives we acquire some good and some bad attitudes.

The last of human freedoms is to choose one's attitude in any given set of circumstances.
Victor Frankl

Victor Frankl, a survivor of the Holocaust, developed this philosophy during his imprisonment in a Nazi concentration camp. He chose to react positively to his situation rather than to justify an attitude of despair.

Faith and a good attitude are inseparable. Where one is found, the other will almost always be found also. Faith is a God-given power locked inside you. The Bible states that God has "dealt to every man the measure of faith" (Rom. 12:3). Your attitude is the key that unlocks that power. If your attitude is right, it will help you to create a balance to your faith.

That is very important in this day when some are off balance. I say these three things about God: 1) He is sensible; 2) He is practical; and 3) He is well-balanced. He is our perfect example.

There have been many times in my life when I realized that my attitude was not what God wanted it to be. Sometimes during a crisis a person's attitude really gets lousy. Only I can control my attitude, with God's help. I can't blame my wife, my family, or the circumstances for my bad attitude.

We need to choose to be positive and react right no matter what happens. We all have the ability to have a good attitude. We are not responsible for the attitudes of those around us, but we are responsible for our own attitude. Those who have a good attitude will usually react to problems differently than those who have a negative attitude.

Sometimes we allow things from our past to mess up our present attitude. When we do this, we are giving up the control that God has granted us.

No one has ever given me a bad attitude. I get it on my own, by allowing what someone else said or did to affect my feelings and my actions. God has given us the power to have a great attitude. God gave us control over our minds, which affects our attitude. Most people I know who have great dreams and high goals also work on having a good attitude.

Your attitude speaks to others. It can say, "*I love you. I think you're important.*" Or it can say, "*I'm jealous of you. I didn't like what you did. I'm tired of my job. I don't like this thing.*" You speak without a sound. Attitudes are mirrors of what we are thinking, and they show up in spite of what we say.

Attitudes for Success

You can know how someone likes his job by his attitude. You can often detect attitude by the tone of a person's voice. It can be seen through his enthusiasm or by a handshake. A person's eyes can reveal much of his attitude by whether or not he meets your gaze directly. The sincerity of a smile reflects attitude. Handwriting also can show attitude. And the manner in which you walk and talk and dress indicates your attitude.

Some of us need to practice having a good attitude. I often have to work on mine. I don't have much patience with the way others do things if I feel they are inept or inefficient. I often have to make a conscious effort to keep a good attitude. I have to tell myself that even if others do things differently from my method, it doesn't matter.

When I'm traveling and my schedule gets messed up, I just say, "It's all part of world travel." Then things seem to run a lot smoother. In a few days it won't matter anyway, so what's the big problem now?

The greatest revelation of our generation is the discovery that human beings, by changing the inner attitudes of their minds, can change the outer aspects of their lives.

William James

Some people have a mental malignancy. Their attitude projects trouble. It projects obstacles. It projects fear, doubt, and pessimism. It is an attitude of worry. It shows a lack of confidence, and it sees failure. These people permit it in their lives.

Never complain about what you permit.

Mike Murdock

Sometimes our pet peeves mess up our attitude. We can keep a good attitude and be free from aggravation if we want to. The decision is ours.

Being judgmental can cause us to get disgusted at others because they don't perform up to our standards of behavior. We need an attitude of understanding for others. We need a shift in the way we think about others and the way they do things.

A Shift in Attitude

Listen to this story. It illustrates a shift in attitude...

You just purchased a brand-new car. You don't want to even leave footprints on the mat. As you drive carefully down the road, you see a small boy waving frantically. As you pass him, he throws something at the car. You hear a noise as a rock hits your fender—he has scratched, maybe dented, your beautiful new car.

You slam on the brakes, back up, jump out, and start toward the child, who is now running toward the house. You follow, determined to give his parents what for. They are going to pay for the damage! Your blood pressure is near boiling. Your attitude is vindictive. You catch up to the kid at the door. He turns. He looks up. You see his tears and fright as he says, "My little brother fell down the stairs. He's really hurt. I'm sorry I hit your car, but I need someone to help me."

What happens to your anger and your high blood pressure? It switches to "Superhero Rescue" mode. Why? Understanding the situation brought a shift in attitude. Your attitude completely changed—what a great kid this big brother is!

When you understand a situation, it will help your attitude. But in order to truly understand, you often have to listen and observe those around you.

The waitress was getting impatient as the little boy tried to decide what he wanted. It was the middle of the lunch rush, and she felt the pressure. "How much is a milkshake?" he asked.

"A dollar and a half," she answered.

"How about a sundae?"

"The same price."

"What about just a dish of ice cream?"

"That's only a dollar twenty-five," was her answer.

"I'll take the ice cream."

She slapped it down unceremoniously. Later, when she returned to clear his place, she discovered a quarter placed neatly under the dish. He had the money for the more expensive items, but he chose not to treat himself to what he really wanted so he would have something to leave as a tip.

Improving Your Attitude

One good way to improve your attitude is to increase your confidence. As a baby, you were confident that your mother would feed you. As an adult you are confident that you will be paid for your work. You believe that your body will heal a cut. You are confident that an umbrella will keep the rain from falling on your head. God's Word is a great confidence builder— get into it!

We also need to learn to control negative expectations. Expectations control our life. Most people seem to believe in negative results. I've heard that 90 percent of adults think negatively, thus causing a bad attitude. Don't worry about what you can't change.

I have a friend, now in her 80's, who has spent much of her life preparing for the worst things to happen in any given situation. Over and over, she seems almost disappointed when things turn out better than she expected.

Since our attitudes are reflected in our lives and expectations, we often receive the negatives that we expect. At one point Job said, "The thing which I greatly feared is come upon me" (Job 3:25a). He expected tragedy.

If all salespeople would have positive attitudes, expecting to sell, their sales would increase. If you ask people to describe their job, their answers usually consist of statements like, *"I work for J.C. Penney; I work for a fertilizer company; I'm in the insurance business; I'm in real estate."* Very few will respond, *"I sell clothing; I sell apples,"* or whatever. Their response is not totally positive. They don't say, *"I expect to make a sale in real estate."* Their attitude of expectation is wrong. God wants us to have an attitude of success.

Three men are working in a rock quarry. The first man says he is breaking rocks. The second man states that he is earning his salary. But the third man says, "I'm building a cathedral." Each man is correct about what he is doing, but the attitude of the third man surely makes it more pleasant to swing the sledgehammer.

No Driver

Now and again you will read that a car crashed because it had no driver. The driver had died at the wheel from a heart attack or whatever. There are a lot of people whose lives "have no driver." They sit in the driver's seat, start the engine, and maybe start down the street, but they "die at the wheel" from a fatal bad attitude. Other lives end before the car is even out of the garage!

A positive attitude will always find a way to achieve the impossible. A person with a good attitude doesn't allow the negative to overwhelm him into quitting. When we change our attitudes from negative to positive, we can change our future. The difference is all in the attitude, and God has given us the power to choose our attitude.

Your attitude is more important than your IQ. It's more important than your past. It's more important than the opinion of others. It's more important than your education and any degrees you may have earned. It's even more important than either finances or present circumstances. And it's more important than the people around us.

A positive attitude does not refuse to recognize problems; rather, it refuses to dwell on those problems. Some have a bad attitude because we live in a negative world, and they have allowed all the ways of this perverted world to infest their attitude. Because of the negative world we live in, our mind can get filled with garbage. It's hard to have a good attitude if our mind is full of garbage.

I don't like it when people dump negative things in my ear. I am not a garbage dump. However, if someone has a problem and wants help, I am there.

There are few things worse than having a bad attitude, and few nicer than having a good attitude. Many times our attitude becomes bad because of circumstances, what others have done, or what's happened to us. Unfortunately, our attitude will be remembered long after those things are forgotten. Our attitude should be like the one Jesus portrayed. (See Philippians 2:5.)

Cause Discovered

When Clare Boothe Luce was appointed as U.S. Ambassador to Italy, she made her home in a beautiful villa built in the seventeenth century. Eventually she began to notice personal physical deterioration. She was tired and began to lose weight, and she had little energy. Her physical condition continued to worsen. She sought medical aid and discovered that she was suffering from arsenic poisoning. Was her staff trying to poison her? Where was this arsenic coming from? All her staff was checked and found to be trustworthy.

Finally the cause was discovered. The ceiling was painted with beautiful roses, but the paint contained arsenic and lead. As a fine dust fell from the roses, it slowly poisoned Mrs. Luce. Sometimes we're unaware of the dangers from the society we live in. Our attitudes and concepts can be poisoned by the materialistic values of those around us. We're often unaware of it until the damage has been done. Don't let satan rearrange your mental furniture and poison you a little at a time until you're destroyed.

Our attitude affects others. My former pastors, Dale and Mary Lou Carpenter, as well as my present pastors, Jon and Melodee Oletzke, have positive attitudes. Thus, the Carpenter's son, Cal, who is also a pastor, has a good attitude. The attitudes of the staff and board at our local church are positive. This in turn reflects to the congregation. None of us are perfect, so there are times when we all have to work on our attitude. Remember that your attitude affects others.

A United Airlines flight attendant once asked me why I was happy and singing all the time. "Are you a Christian?" she queried.

"Of course," I answered affirmatively.

"I knew it," she said. "Your attitude shows it."

You have an opportunity to discover God today in a way you have never discovered Him.

Peter Doseck

Notes

1. Work on your attitude now!

2. Forget who did what to you.

3. Stop predicting problems.

Top Three Changes to Make!

1.

2.

3.

Chapter Four

Challenges and Obstacles

Sometimes we make big things out of nothing. A lady came up to me one day, extremely upset. She declared, "I don't like your beard."

"That's fine," I answered.

"Why do you grow a beard, anyway?" she continued.

Now, I could have gotten upset and told her that it was none of her business and that I didn't like her hair. But I decided to stay sweet and turn this challenge into a stepping-stone. I said, "Let me tell you what happened and one reason that I have the beard. I used to shave every day. I would cut it off, but the next morning God grew it out again. This went on for several years until I finally said to God, 'Okay, God, if You want to grow it out, there it is,' and I just let Him grow it out."

She had no answer to this reasoning, and we laughed together. Now, every time I see her, she says, "I see God is still in control."

I tell this story as a humorous illustration that sometimes we take little things that don't really matter and make them bigger than they really are. We blow them all out of proportion and get into trouble because of it.

You don't go by what everything looks like. You have to go by what God's Word says, and trust God.

Happy Caldwell

It seems that our lives are always under construction. We keep going through construction zones and getting held up on our journey. We're always having to rebuild a road, replace a bridge, or repave the surface. The construction areas of our life are filled with challenges and obstacles that sometimes grow into crises if we allow them to. At this very moment it doesn't matter how discouraged you are; you can get through it. Turn this discouraging situation into an opportunity. God says, "I know the plans I have for you...plans to prosper you and not to harm you, plans to give you hope and a future" (Jer. 29:11 NIV). You should be more than excited to think of what God has planned for you!

Great victories come out of great battles.
Smith Wigglesworth

Those who finally succeed are the ones who use challenges and setbacks as opportunities. They assess the situation and then move forward. They don't accept challenges as permanent obstacles that will curse them forever. Setbacks don't keep them from trying again. They know failure is only temporary. They use the setback as a stepping-stone to a positive future.

*I*f *you want a place in the sun, you have to put up with a few blisters.*

Abigail Van Buren

Your challenges are only opportunities with a few thorns. Having an inner peace in your life comes from God. Patience also comes only from God. During a challenge, inner peace and patience ensure progress through the challenge. "You will keep him in perfect peace, whose mind is stayed on You, because he trusts in You" (Is. 26:3 NKJV). Live in harmony with God, and His peace will flood your life.

*S*ome *of us let those great dreams die, but others nourish and protect them, nurse them through bad days 'til they bring them to sunshine and light which comes always.*

Woodrow Wilson

I used to think that it was the impatient people who accomplished great things. I have discovered that I was wrong. Impatient people will get things started, but it's the patient people who actually see things through to completion. They remain calm through the waiting period. They are able to ignore the turbulence. They live above it and keep a great attitude.

*F*aith *opens the door to God's promise for you, and patience keeps it open until that promise is fulfilled.*

Kenneth Copeland

Noah Webster spent 36 years working on his dictionary. Edison failed 10,000 times in his efforts to perfect the lightbulb.

Fannie Hurst received 36 rejections from the *Saturday Evening Post* before her first story was accepted for publication. Sir Isaac Newton spent nearly 40 years before writing his law of gravity. He stated, "What I have done is due to patient thought."

T*he battle belongs to the persistent. Refuse to let friends or circumstances defeat you.*

Van Crouch

Patience

Maybe you are wondering what patience has to do with obstacles and challenges. I think that patience has to be involved with overcoming these things. The next time you face a tremendous challenge or crisis in your life, try one of these two prayers.

The first one was written by Dr. Reinhold Niebuhr in 1935. It was adopted by Alcoholics Anonymous, and the USO distributed it to American soldiers during World War II.

O God, give me the serenity to accept what cannot be changed,
the courage to change what should be changed,
and wisdom to distinguish one from the other.

The second one was written more than 400 years ago by Saint Teresa of Avila.

Let nothing disturb thee, let nothing dismay thee, all things pass.
God never changes. Patience attains all that it strives for.
He who has God finds he lacks nothing. God alone suffices.

When you face a challenge or hit an obstacle of some kind with another person, there are three possible solutions.

1. *The first option is to change the other person.* It might be a very big problem to try to change his thinking—and that can lead to even bigger problems. Books have been written on how to change the other guy, but such a task can be difficult to impossible. Think about the last time somebody tried to change you!

2. *The second solution is to change the situation.* Avoid coming into contact with the person who is causing the problem. Some people feel that quitting the job or moving out of the neighborhood is the answer to their problem. However, this may not be solving the problem—you may just be taking it with you.

3. *The third solution is to change yourself.* This is probably the most satisfactory answer. Change your way of looking at the thing. Exhibit a desire to change. Change your attitude.

I *will go anywhere, as long as it is upward.*
David Livingstone

When the 911 emergency calling first came out, we were all excited. Now we could actually get help if we needed it. God also has a "911" we can call when in need. The psalmist says in Psalm 91:1, "He that dwelleth in the secret place of the most High shall abide under the shadow of the Almighty."

Having a right relationship with God, the source of all our answers, will change you. You will become more like Him.

Notes

1. Do not make big things out of little things. Most things are little things.

2. Live above discouragement.

3. Realize that any challenge is an opportunity in the making.

4. Practice patience.

Top Three Changes to Make!

1.

2.

3.

Chapter Five

Opportunities

God-given opportunities knock at our door. They often appear in different forms and come from different directions than we expect. That is one of the tricks of opportunity. It comes in the back door disguised as defeat, and it often goes unrecognized because of its disguise.

> **P**roblems are only opportunities in work clothes.
>
> **Henry J. Kaiser**

Thomas Edison invented the "Edison Dictating Machine." His sales representatives had a hard time generating enthusiasm for the thing. They felt that it would take too much effort to develop a market for it. This opportunity was hidden in a weird-looking machine. But a Mr. Barnes saw the opportunity. He was sure that he could sell it. Edison agreed to give him a chance. Barnes sold so many of the machines that Edison gave him a contract to distribute them. As a result, Barnes became rich. He proved that it could happen. He grabbed an opportunity and fulfilled its potential.

I believe that the biggest cause of failure is quitting before the opportunity takes hold. Don't quit just because someone tells you it can't be done. There are always "dream destroyers" out to knock you down. They can really fog your vision. You need a clear vision and a strong sense of purpose in order to recognize good opportunities, and God gave us the ability to recognize them and achieve success. Success occurs when we take opportunities, and failures happen when we miss them.

Opportunities are usually disguised as hard work, so most people don't recognize them.

Ann Landers

People don't always understand the things they see or hear. My parents often said things that I didn't understand. They would tell me that I "couldn't get something for nothing." Later they'd say that "the best things in life are free."

Only he who can see the invisible can do the impossible.

Richard Roberts

Dad would tell me, "I don't want to spank you." My answer was, "Don't do it, then." Sometimes he would ask, "Do you want some more?" Imagine me answering, "Sure, do it again. I like it!"

Mom would tell us, "Don't go near the water until you learn how to swim." We had to practice in the rain.

Once she told us, "We're having company. You kids eat with your mouths closed." I wrote her a note asking, "How will I get the food in?"

Opportunities

It's been said that whatever the mind can conceive can be achieved. We need to make use of our opportunities.

Moses saw the invisible, chose the imperishable, and did the impossible. Don't miss out on opportunities just because they don't seem to be practical.

You need clear vision, a strong sense of purpose, and determination in order to really recognize opportunities.

Notes

1.   Pray about opportunities.

2.   Once you take an opportunity, don't let go when it gets hard to handle.

Top Three Changes to Make!

1.

2.

3.

Chapter Six

Successes and Failures

L et's start by defining both of these terms, *success* and *failure*. *Success* is the ability to complete the projects that one starts. Success is often defined by material possessions, but it is more than that. True success in life is measured by what a person is, not by what a person has. Likewise, *failure* is failing to seek to do and be all God wants us to do and be. God is not glorified when we fail in this way. Failure is falling down and refusing to get up.

Historically, wherever the gospel is preached and practiced, the lifestyle of those who embrace it is elevated. There can be periods of persecution and hardship that temporarily interrupt this pattern, but because of the higher standard of morality and ethics, a higher standard of living is the eventual effect.

However, because the world places such an emphasis on material success, the concept of a Christian succeeding has been given bad press in some circles. That may be because most people in our material world don't really know what success is. To some, success means wealth, a big house, lots of cars, and no need to work. Success seems elusive because we measure it by what others have achieved. When we see someone in a big fancy car, we often remark—or at least think—how successful that person must be. When we hear of someone traveling the world, we feel that person must be successful.

Success has nothing to do with what you gain or accomplish for yourself. It's what you do for others.

Danny Thomas

The Bible contains numerous admonitions against becoming obsessed with the pursuit of money. We are never to love money so much that we lose concern for spiritual values or care less about and for others around us.

Rich or poor, we are strongly instructed to be good stewards of whatever God entrusts to us. Taken by themselves, the statements that the apostle Paul makes about contentment (See Phil. 4:11-12; 1 Tim. 6:6) may seem to be instructing readers to be apathetic in every area of life. I seriously doubt that Paul intended that we sit on the sidelines and make no effort to succeed. Paul must have been an extremely busy, vigorous individual, judging by what he accomplished for God.

When we succeed, we enjoy the adulation of those around us. When we really need encouragement, not as many are found who are ready to offer that encouragement. No one likes to be around what they consider to be a failure.

Fear has a lot to do with failure. Keep in mind that success and God's blessing on your life and future will never jump out and attack you. You can't be afraid to fail. People who have succeeded in anything in life have recognized the causes for their failures. On the other hand, many great dreams have been destroyed because of a single failure. But we can take failures and turn them into successes by putting God first in our lives.

Turn your scars into stars.

Robert Schuller

We have to really desire success in our lives in order to attain it. Many failures are due to weak wills. God gave us a will to succeed. It's nearly impossible to succeed without that will. The will to succeed takes us out of failure and uses failure as a stepping-stone on the road to success. It will take a nervous, discontented, timid person and transform him into a dynamo.

The Lord gave us two ends, one to sit on and one to think with. Success depends on which one we use most.

Ann Landers

You can go to the uncrowded world of success and find that most people there have taken failures and turned them into successes. They come from all backgrounds, financial strata, and walks of life. They may be rich or poor, good or bad, tall or short, heavy or skinny, from all parts of the world, and with different cultural and ethnic origins. What they have in common is that they took failure and made it into success. Those who really want to succeed view failure as a temporary setback.

---

*A*bsorb *the principle that failure is never final, so if you do not succeed the first time, keep on trying.*

Daisy Osborn

That's good news for us. Every time we fail, we can salvage something from the failure and use it to build toward success.

Decide to do it. It doesn't matter what goes wrong—whether it's in church, in your business, on your job, at home, or with your car—you can make it a stepping-stone. When we succeed, we want everybody to know. But when we fail, we tend to pull back into a shell; we don't want others to know. At times like those, true friends will come and lift you up and help see you through. Others may call you a loser and not offer to help because they believe you are whipped. They may even tell others that you gave up.

When you tell yourself that you're whipped, you lose the ability to conquer the problem. You will feel whipped, act whipped, and stop trying. When you say that you can do it, it becomes God talking through you. You feel that you can make it. You can succeed.

Look at your setbacks and turn them into pavement on your road to success. Assess your weaknesses and mistakes, look things over, and decide where you need to change. Begin to make those changes. Try a different route. Look at the bright side. Trust God to help you find a better way to attack the situation. Go to the true source of your success.

---

*W*inners *are ex-losers who got mad.*

Van Crouch

Motivation

Sometimes the difference between success and failure is motivation. Some people are happy in life while others are always disgruntled. If we want to turn our failures around, we need a positive motivation. It will move us to make things happen.

Well-motivated people have purpose, direction, and energy. They have whatever it takes to make it happen. They know success is imminent. Without motivation you will remain a failure and never find the answer. If you are motivated to succeed, failure will never hold you back. You believe that "all things are possible" (Mk. 9:23). You believe that it will work. You know that failure is only temporary, and you are motivated to succeed.

To be truly successful, you need to believe in God. Success is not necessarily a huge thing. It is basically two things: 1) *knowing what God wants you to do, and* 2) *doing it.*

When Billy Graham comes to a city, he draws the attention of the news media. Traffic on the freeways and side roads becomes snarled as his crusade draws huge crowds of people. Thousands make decisions for Christ. He is a success.

A missionary to Alaska travels for days by dogsled to minister in a village of maybe ten people. All of them find Christ. He is just as successful as Billy Graham. Each has done what God asked him to do.

When we understand why we have failed, it's easier to go on to success. We need to understand certain things. When my grandkids were small, we played "make-believe monsters." I would knock on the door or under the table and say, "Uh-oh, monsters!" Their eyes would get big as we all looked around for the monster. We all knew it was a game. After a while, they discovered that Papa was the monster and there was no need to be afraid. We had a lot of fun. I wish we could deal with our adult monsters as easily as the grandkids and I did.

Real and pretend are nearly interchangeable for a small child. Unfortunately, adults can confuse the two as well. Many people carry monsters of failure around that keep them from succeeding. They have unfounded feelings of worthlessness, worry, fear, unforgiveness, and other negative emotions that rob them of their ability to reach success.

Surveys have been conducted that asked people what they wanted most from life. People list many things. The top items they want are 1) success, 2) health, 3) happiness, and 4) recognition. Love ranks only fifth.

A simple lust for money is wrong, but a desire to have resources in order to be able to give and bless others is acceptable.

An attitude of failure is contagious—others can catch it from us. Parents can pass it on unwittingly to their children when they say things like, "You're such a mess," or "Why can't you ever do things right?" or even "Why can't you be like [name of sibling]?" They don't realize that they are programming the child to failure.

In the story of Gideon (see Judg. 6–7), God shows that less is sometimes more. He had Gideon send almost 32,000 men home. Then, with a band of only 300, Gideon slew the mighty Midianite army, which numbered more than 100,000.

John Avanzini and I were discussing failure and success over breakfast in Jerusalem. He told me, "Success and failure are a unique situation. The two greatest disappointments in life are 1) not to accomplish your heart's desires, and 2) not to accomplish your heart's desires because the 'carrot' that kept you moving is gone."

Failure *is not failing to meet your goal. Real failure is failure to reach as high as you possibly can.*

Robert Schuller

Failure is a spirit from hell that will destroy you. Victory comes from Heaven and will lift you up. The Lord says in Jeremiah 1:8, "Be not afraid of their faces: for I am with thee to deliver thee." He will take us from failure to success. "Fear ye not, stand still, and see the salvation of the Lord" (Ex. 14:13b). "When thou goest out to battle...be not afraid...for the Lord thy God is with thee" (Deut. 20:1).

God promised to take us through whatever the circumstances are and lead us to victory. God wants you to win when you battle against failure. No problem can stand against God's victory in your life. Don't look at the size of the problem. It may seem much bigger than you are. Through God, you will succeed. You will be victorious. You will be successful; you are not under the curse of failure. You are under the blessing of God when you put Him first in your life.

No *man will ever truly know that he has succeeded until he has experienced an apparent failure.*

Robert Schuller

Too many people fear failure. It haunts them day and night. It fills their mind with fear. It causes them to lack the confidence that God has placed within them what they need to be a success.

Some people will try to destroy your confidence. They want you to fail. But John wrote, "Greater is He that is in you, than he that is in the world" (1 Jn. 4:4). How can you overcome the fear of failure? Jesus said, "If ye continue in My word...ye shall know the truth, and the truth shall make you free" (Jn. 8:31-32).

Psalm 112:7-8 tells us that when we trust the Lord, we will not be afraid. We stand on the Word of God. Jesus said that if we abide (or remain) in Him and His words abide in us, then we shall ask whatever we wish, and it shall be done for us (see Jn. 15:7). That doesn't sound like failure to me; it sounds like success.

Dream Big Dreams and Trust a Big God

You are more than a conqueror through Him that loved you (see Rom. 8:37). God has built a shield around you; failure cannot enter in there. You are going on to be a success because that is what God desires for you in every avenue of your life.

Quit looking at past failures. Disregard fears and frustrations. Start believing the Word of God. Allow yourself to become rooted in victory and success in your life. God is your strength and your power. Say this aloud numerous times each day: "*God is my strength and my power. I'm going to believe God. Fear is not to be in me. Perfect love casts out fear. I will not let satan invade my soul. I will stop agreeing with the devil. He has no legal right to make me a failure. God will make me a success.*"

If you are one of those people who say they don't believe in talking positive, then go ahead and talk negative and be a failure. God wants us to talk positive. We are victorious because He is victorious. We will triumph because He triumphs. We have the answer because He is the answer. We will win because He is a winner and makes us a winner. Our lives are successful because God made us to be successful. We were born to be successful, to overcome satan and failure. It is all part of having that personal relationship with the living God.

David said he wouldn't be afraid. "In God have I put my trust: I will not be afraid what man can do unto me" (Ps. 56:11).

You can laugh at your failures and say, *"Satan, I am making my failure a stepping-stone. I will achieve and succeed like God wants me to. I've stepped on failure, fear, frustration, and anxiety and made them stepping-stones."* That's how we climb the ladder to the answer God has for us. John wrote, "I wish above all things that thou mayest prosper and be in health..." (3 Jn. 2).

I have strong confidence in God that He wants me to be a total success in every area of my life. I have faith in Him, and I stand on His Word. I am an overcomer. It will happen.

You need to say, *"The failure spirit is out of my life."* Failure comes when you yield to a spirit of failure. Instead, rejoice and be happy. Believe that God will see you through. When failure strikes or trouble comes, laugh at it and thank God for future successes.

Failure *is never final, and success is never-ending.*

Robert Schuller

We often believe that because we failed before, we will do so again. We need to laugh at the problem, the apparent failure. Have a wonderful time. God is fixing to bless you. You're going to cross the Red Sea and not fail the test. Worship God; refuse to allow a spirit of failure to get hold of you. Rise above those problems, failures, and frustrations and begin to rejoice in the Lord.

Your apparent failure is not really your problem. Your ignorance of why the failure occurred is the real problem. When you learn to trust God, you know that He will bring victory to you and make you a success. The circumstances don't matter because God is bigger than the circumstances. He's bigger than the negatives around you that tear at your faith. You may be fearful of failure; negative circumstances may push you, but you can rebuke the circumstances just like Jesus rebuked the wind and the sea.

F*or me, success is...to leave the woodpile a little higher than I found it.*

Paul Harvey

Maybe you have some problem that you feel is a major thing in your life, but none of us has to worry: God will fight our battles. We can come boldly before God and trust Him without worry. But it's up to us. We can choose whether to yield to failure or to God. I sleep well at night because I give all my problems to the Lord—He's awake all night anyway.

Abraham and Sarah were childless. They were concerned about their situation, because it looked like a failure. When they tried to correct the situation on their own, the result was Ishmael's birth. God's miracle child, Isaac, finally came in spite of their efforts, not because of them. When we try to do it our own way, we often get into trouble.

Do you fear failure? Give everything over to God. Let God make havoc of the enemy. When Abraham took his mind off the circumstances, when he and Sarah quit worrying about their old age, a miracle happened. They went from failure to success. God is your refuge also. Tell yourself that daily.

I try to be so conditioned by God's Word that I refuse to fail. The devil may try to sidetrack me, but I will keep my confidence in God. I believe that I will have victory. The battle—and the victory—are the Lord's. (See First Samuel 17:47.)

The Bible is full of examples of God's turning seeming defeat into victory. Stumbling doesn't mean defeat. Refusing to get up and try again is what makes for defeat.

Do you have time to succeed, or are you so busy failing that success is impossible? You will never float into success. It won't sneak up on you, hit you on the head, or jump out of a tree and scare you. It won't even happen just because you attend the right seminars. With a dream, a plan, and a goal, plus hard work and a heart right with God, it will happen.

Failure is an opportunity to begin again, this time more intelligently.

Henry Ford

Notes

1.   Start trusting God for success.

2.   Take any failure and turn it into a success.

3.   Stay positively motivated.

4.   Remember, success is:
     a.   Knowing what God wants you to do.
          AND
     b.   Doing it.

Top Three Changes to Make!

1.

2.

3.

Chapter Seven

Family and Home

In First Corinthians 13 (often called the love chapter), in the Amplified Bible, we are told that love never points out the faults or past failures of others in our family, nor is critical of them. Sometimes we don't do the right thing with our family, with our own children. I wish I had time to re-live my children's growing-up years. I don't think I held them in my arms enough or prayed with them like I should have. I should have reached out and touched them; I should have showed them that I cared, more than I did. Barbara and I married young and had our children early, so we all basically grew up together.

Mark 10:13-16 tells us of the love that Jesus showed to children. He admonished the disciples to be more childlike. Jesus wasn't uptight with children; He picked them up and blessed them. We often become impatient with the immaturity of children. Their noise and mess upset our adult sensibilities.

Re-Arranging Your Mental Furniture

I love the book, *Making Your Home a Home* by Billy Joe Daugherty. He offers these "ten commandments" for parents that help us improve our relationship with our children. They are listed below, along with some of my own thoughts and experiences.

1. *"Thou shalt start with thyself."* Parents need to set an example for their children to follow. We can't tell them to do something that we are not doing ourselves. One time my daughter, Becki, was trying to teach the grandkids to sit down to eat, but we adults were standing and walking around the lunchroom. We can't tell them one thing and do another.

2. *"Thou shalt be more concerned about relationships than rules."* We all have rules. We can't totally eliminate them. Rules and guidelines are necessary. But we have to build a relationship, and we have to love our children as we build a relationship that should model the relationship we want them to have with their heavenly Father.

3. *"Thou shalt impart the faith."* We need to discuss spiritual things with our children. Age-appropriate Bible reading and stories are a must. Teach them very early to pray and to love God and the things of God. (See Deuteronomy 6:5-9.)

4. *"Thou shalt learn to listen."* My wife was better at this than I was. Our children listen to us more readily when we take the time to listen to them also. Listening is not easy; most of us would rather talk. Instead of listening, we are usually just waiting for a pause when we can add our own input.

5. *"Thou shalt spend time with thy children."* That has always been hard for me. For years, I felt that my "ministry" was more important than my family. There didn't seem to be enough time to do the things that I felt were important, and taking time from the family seemed to be the easiest way to get

more time for what I felt needed to be done. God had to change some of my priorities.

We need to build relationships while our kids are small if we want good communication when they are grown. I often regret that I didn't take more time for fun with them when they were growing up. I know that I frequently neglected our daughter, Becki, because I felt that girls should be with their mother and boys with their father. I didn't realize how wrong this was. I was stuck in the traditional idea that boys did boy things and girls did girl things. I didn't realize until much later how much resentment Becki built up because of my seeming favoritism for our sons, Nathan and Dan. Now, however, Becki is a major part of the ministry. She is extremely efficient, and I can always trust her to make the right decision.

6. *"Thou shalt acknowledge thy faults as a parent."* (See James 5:16.) We hate to say that we're sorry, that we made a mistake. We hate to ask our children to forgive us. It just isn't in us. Aren't we supposed to be in charge?

7. *"Thou shalt keep a sense of humor."* That's easy for me. A merry heart does good like medicine, the Bible says in Proverbs 17:22.

8. *"Thou shalt treat thy children equally."* I've already told you about my error with mine. Even though you can't always treat them identically, because they are not alike, you can treat them equally.

9. *"Thou shalt use discipline."* This is extremely important. We don't abuse them, but there must be consequences to negative behaviors.

10. *"Thou shalt know when to let go."* One of the best things you can do for your children is teach them how to get along

without you. It's hard to imagine them as adults with abilities of their own. Our son Dan is an intelligent young man. He has a lot of ability and is a great part of our ministry. He has many great ideas, and he is constantly surprising me. I have to be careful that I don't still look at him as a child. He is our vice president and serves on our board!

God intended that the family be the basic unit of society. It is within the framework of family relationships that we learn how to deal with society in general. There are so many attacks on the home and the family today. In First Peter 3, Peter gives us insight into family relationships. I'm praying for my family— not only for my children, but also for my siblings and parents.

If America is going to survive...it will be because husbands and fathers again place their families at the highest level of their system of priorities.

James Dobson

We need to accept each other for who we are and love each other whether or not we always agree. The degree of success that each has or has not achieved should not enter into our relationships as family. We must love each other in spite of our imperfections. If we can feel accepted within our own family, it is much easier to face the challenges that the rest of the world places before us.

You do not lead by hitting people over the head. That's assault, not leadership.

Dwight D. Eisenhower

Communication

Good communication within a family is essential. Did you ever wonder what causes quarrels within a family? They are usually over unimportant things. People get on edge. Dinner is late. Someone speaks without thinking, or someone misinterprets what was said. Voices are raised. Accusations are made in the heat of an argument, and feelings get hurt. Other family members take sides.

Things are rarely settled by quarreling. Petty things get blown out of proportion. How can these conflicts be resolved? Does it really matter that the cap was left off the toothpaste? Or that someone didn't rinse out the bathtub? Or lift the seat? Or hang the towel straight? Do things like these really matter? Learn to be cool and calm.

Confusion and strife hinder God from answering our prayers. Family arguments and disagreements should be settled quickly so our bad feelings don't hinder our relationship with God.

Under Attack

Your home and family are under attack by satan. He knows who you are and where you live, what car you drive and what your weakest points are. God also knows about you and your family. Remember that the blood of Jesus Christ protects you. Satan can't read your mind; he only knows what you say. That's why words are so important. Satan will jump on your words like a chicken on a June bug. However, only God knows the thoughts and intents of your heart—and God can protect your family. Believe it. Act on His Word.

Notes

1. Plan to be a better parent.

2. Believe the fact that God wants to bless your home and family.

3. Work on better communication.

Top Three Changes to Make!

1.

2.

3.

Chapter Eight

Decisions

Your entire life rises or falls on the decisions you make. It is important to make right decisions in our lives—and these decisions should be based on positive values and principles. Putting God first in our life is a major decision. One of the best decisions we can make is to live by Matthew 6:33, in which Jesus says, "Seek ye first the kingdom of God, and His righteousness."

Study the life of the prophet, Daniel. The Bible says he "purposed in his heart that he would not defile himself" (Dan. 1:8a). The easy road would have been to keep quiet and simply eat the food that was offered to him. But Daniel was determined to serve the living God. Because he put God first, God blessed and prospered him. He became one of the highest-ranking officials in the country, and he served under four different kings from three different nations.

You can decide to move on to success or fall back on failure. It's all your decision. Just base all your decisions on positive values.

67

Making a decision often can involve risk. You may have to take a stand for what you really believe, and that might cost you something. When your values are in place and your principles are in order, it's easier to make the right decision. Your future will be blessed by your correct decisions. Remember, success or failure is your choice.

However, even Christians make mistakes. Some make wrong decisions based upon what they *think* God's Word means. Some have bad attitudes because of how they have been thinking, and thus they fail to make right decisions.

T*he only thing that stands between a person and what he wants from life is often the will to try it and the faith to believe that it is possible.*
Richard M. DeVos

To make an accurate decision, you must have accurate facts. Then decide that you can make it happen. Decide that you will carry through.

W*hen I've heard all I need to know to make a decision, I don't take a vote, I make a decision.*
Ronald Reagan

The Plan

Before we go anywhere, we first have to decide where we are going. Then we plan the mode of transportation and the route. Will we drive or fly? What vehicle will get us to our destination? Once we decide on the vehicle, we get into it. We check the fuel supply. Then we start the vehicle, put it in gear, take our foot off the brake, and step on the accelerator. We follow the route to our destination.

We can't drive from here to London because of the ocean in between; we have to fly. Similarly, there is no possible way for our life to have meaning unless we follow the right directions. And our route book is the Bible.

In order to accomplish something, we must first know what we want to accomplish. We need to know where we want to go. If you're just out for a pleasure ride with no destination in mind, don't blame anyone else if you don't make much progress. Circumstances won't take you to success if you aren't heading in the right direction.

We also have to get and follow good directions on our trip. It's hard to drive to someplace in Kansas if we're using a map of London.

So decide on your destination; set your goal. Then decide how fast you want to get there and what map you will follow. You may be surprised at how much you are able to accomplish. The Bible is our road map.

What you get by reaching your destination isn't really as important as who you become by reaching that destination.
"Zig" Ziglar

When you decide what it is you want out of life, or what your goals are, plan your route. A big goal must often be broken into smaller goals. But you are the one who must decide. In a survey of about 25,000 people who had experienced some kind of failure, they gave one major cause for their failure: a lack of decision.

When we don't make decisions, we tend to procrastinate. When we have decided what we want, we usually go after it. Make the decision to be on God's side.

Eagles, Sparrows, and Pigeons

The eagle portrays the part of us that contacts God. The *Encyclopedia Britannica* tells us that since ancient times, eagles have been used as symbols of empire, courage, and military prowess. When we think of an eagle, we think of a bird that flies way up high with little effort. The bald eagle was adopted as the emblem of the United States, probably because of the ancient use of the symbol, and also because of the bird's magnificent majesty in flight—an almost effortless mastery of its majestic art.

Everyone who knows me knows that I love eagles. My office is filled with all kinds of eagles in brass, wood, glass, and photos. They intrigue me. I have watched them in flight until they disappeared into the distance. You rarely see an eagle do much wing flapping. It makes a few flaps of its wings until it gets into an updraft, then it relaxes and allows the wind to do the work, continuing to climb with each circle. It seems so effortless. God wants us to think like the eagle—to function like it and reach great altitudes of answered prayer.

I'm afraid that too often we function like sparrows, digging in the dirt and making a lot of commotion, but not getting very far. When Jesus told us to consider the sparrow, He was referring to the fact that there are a lot of them—they are a dime a dozen. (See Luke 12:6-7.) Sparrows are not interested in great heights. They are looking for bugs and stirring up dust.

Some people function like pigeons, hanging out in groups and making a great noise, but only leaving a mess. They love the sound of their own voices. At the first sound of danger, they take off in seemingly organized panic, circle for a short time, then return, busy at making noise again. Their actions accomplish little. We shouldn't function like sparrows or pigeons. God wants us to mount up on wings as eagles (see Is. 40:31).

In my years of traveling, I've seen many things in many churches. Some churches seem to be doing all the right things, but without much in the way of results. Some pastors minister with great-sounding sermons that cause no change in people's lives. Others use psychology and humanism, but nothing happens. Life is more than going through the motions. We need to soar like the eagle, letting the Holy Spirit lead us into the presence of God. Again, it's our relationship to God that causes us to succeed.

Our relationship to God is our source for the power we need to overcome. Satan, on the other hand, will try to attack us and blame us for everything. This brings a story to mind.

Sam and Joe always seemed to be in the middle of every bit of mischief that happened, both at school and around home. Their parents reached a place where they were at their wits' end. So they decided to take the boys to see their pastor.

Joe went into the pastor's office while Sam sat outside by the door. The pastor paced back and forth in front of Joe. Finally, he looked the boy in the eye and asked, "Son, where is God?" The child just stared at him.

"I said, 'Where is God?' " he repeated. Still no answer.

He bent down until his face was even with that of Joe and asked again, forcefully, "Where is God?"

This time Joe jumped to his feet and ran out the door. He ran past the startled Sam, who asked what had happened.

"Let's get out of here quick!" cried Joe. "God's missing, and they think we have something to do with it!"

Satan will always throw blame at us, but with the power of God, we can defeat him.

W*e trust...that God is on our side. However, it is more important that we are on God's side.*

Abraham Lincoln

Notes

1. Make decisions based on the Bible.

2. Once you decide, follow through.

3. Ask God to forgive you for wrong decisions you've made in the past.

Top Three Changes to Make!

1.

2.

3.

Chapter Nine

Health and Healing

Even when a person really wants to do something, he or she will often use bad health as an excuse for failure. I need to say here that the state of our health is not an indication of our spirituality; neither is the fact of being rich or poor a good barometer of our spiritual condition.

Many doctors say that everyone has something physically wrong with them. Some people use that as an excuse. People sometimes even imagine ailments and as a result actually develop symptoms because they are worrying about it. Statistics tell us that three out of every four hospital beds are filled with someone who has an emotionally induced illness. If people would learn how to handle their emotions, they would get well sooner.

I've done a lot of research and discussed this issue with several doctors. I am convinced that many of the illnesses people suffer are either caused or made worse by their associating with others who talk about how badly they look, how serious their condition is, and who they know who died from the same illness.

A friend of mine had an arm amputated. His attitude was that while he liked having two arms better, one arm and a good spirit were better than two arms and a bad spirit. His spirit was complete.

I don't think that people should worry, talk, and complain about their health. We should just thank God that it's as good as it is. Let's look for improvement!

Having good health is, for many of us, a decision-making process—at least to a point. You can decide to be healthy by eating correctly and getting proper sleep and exercise. God wants our bodies to be in good health. It is easier to maintain good health than it is to cure an illness. Good health is important.

Suppose you decide to eat a piece of celery. That food has no mind of its own, but your body is so created that it takes the nutrients in that food and uses them for the things it needs, such as healing a cut. An open wound appears to heal by itself. But God created us so that the necessary cells would go to that area and cause the tissues to regenerate. (Still, this healing puts a lot of stress on the rest of your body.)

Bad health is a big negative for your life. If you want to be healthy, do the things that make you healthy: Eat a balanced diet, exercise, and get enough rest.

S ome people wonder why they can't have faith for healing. They feed their bodies three hot meals a day and their spirits one cold snack a week.

F.F. Bosworth

Symptoms

Don't be always looking for adverse symptoms. Don't expect illness to come or to recur. Don't talk yourself into feeling down and depressed. Reject the thought that you are getting sick. Have confidence that God wants you to be healthy. Think and talk about good health. Act alive.

There can be times when very well-meaning friends and family will "sympathize" with us. Nevertheless, their kindness and caring can have a negative effect on our attitude, and we can actually let them talk us into feeling worse than we do. Don't let that happen.

God made your body, and He doesn't make junk. Be confident that your body will serve you well. Resist sickness, disease, and germs. Use common sense and cleanliness. Some microbes are beneficial, needed for digestion and other body functions. Others carry disease. Frequent hand washing during an epidemic of colds and flu is only good judgment. It's not being paranoid.

In order to be in health and have energy, live a clean, well-balanced life—and work toward that end. Avoid unnecessary stress, which tends to weaken the immune system.

When I pray for people, I often ask God to make their body function the way He wants it to function. His Word states that it is His desire that we be in health (see 3 Jn. 2).

Because of sin, sickness and defects have entered into the picture. But God has promised to heal us when we do get sick. Those promises are our rightful, legal inheritance from God through Jesus Christ.

Some people feel that perhaps God wants them to be sick, that He sends illness. But according to the Word, Jesus took the stripes before His crucifixion in order that we might be healed (see Is. 53:5).

Hosea 4:6 states that God's people "are destroyed for lack of knowledge." They don't know that God wants to heal them. The Bible doesn't say, "I am the Lord who makes you sick"! It says, "I am the Lord that healeth thee" (Ex. 15:26b). Healing is a blessing from God. God's Word promises us healing. God said that healing is one of His benefits: "He sent His word, and healed them" (Ps. 107:20a; see also Ps. 103:3). He said that He would take sickness away from the midst of us (see Deut. 7:15).

If God had wanted people to be sick, Jesus wouldn't have gone around preaching and healing the sick when He was here on earth. To do so would have been to go against His Father. Jesus asked the man at the pool of Bethesda, "Do you want to be well?" Then He told him to pick up his mat and walk (see Jn. 5:2-9). Jesus delivered people and put their lives back together.

Some might ask, then, why we have doctors, nurses, and hospitals. They are also trying to help those who are sick to get well again. I'm not against the medical profession. All healing comes from God, who often uses health care professionals as His instruments to bring about healing.

In John 10:10, Jesus says that He came that we might have life, and that more abundantly. It's hard to enjoy life when we are sick. It is God's will for us to be well, not sick. God is a positive personality, and our faith allows Him to act on our behalf. God doesn't want us to die before our time, like a rotten apple falling from a tree. He wants us well!

On the other hand, satan's negative personality can be activated in our life by our fears. Satan doesn't heal; he only makes people sick.

Health and Healing

God sent His Word and healed people. He brought healing to families. Jesus' ministry was to heal and help. If we resist the devil, he will flee from us (see Jas. 4:7). Sickness and disease have to go.

Notes

1. Believe that your health should be good.

2. Exercise and eat right.

3. Believe that healing is yours (if you're sick). It's been paid for once; don't pay again.

Top Three Changes to Make!

1.

2.

3.

Chapter Ten

Finances

As soon as I begin to discuss money and how God has more than enough for us, I know that I am going to lose some folks. Let me tell you, we are not "in it for the money." At the same time, we all need money in order to function in this world.

Jesus spent a lot of time teaching about money, and He even used it as an illustration in some of His parables.

How we think about money is important. God used people with tremendous wealth all through the Bible. Adam ruled over tremendous wealth. Then sin came in, causing Adam and Eve to lose the prosperity that God wanted them to have. They were evicted from the Garden.

When our relationship with God, the source of all wealth, is right, He supplies our needs. Keep in mind that He doesn't just drop it down on us from Heaven; He works through people. He gives people the strength to work so that they can get a paycheck. He blesses others with the ability to run a business so they can pay people for their work.

The world system we live in requires money. We need housing—and houses cost money. We eat food—and food also costs money. We require transportation and clothing. We want entertainment, etc. You get the picture.

The Bible doesn't say that Jesus had no finances. His group of disciples included a treasurer, so He must have had something that needed to be accounted for. You need to allow God to bless you financially so that you can be a blessing to others and to the work of God.

---

*A*ll of us must become better informed. It is necessary for us to learn from the mistakes of others. We are not going to live long enough to make them all ourselves.

Hyman G. Rickover

Some say, *"God wants me poor,"* or, *"Does God really want me to have money?"* I believe that God is raising up a new generation of people in this time who will believe Him, who will be action-oriented, who have holy boldness and purpose. Their thinking will change. They will believe God and change their world.

When I found out that God is not need-oriented but supply-oriented, it changed my life. God wants to bless us, but I really believe that God will not give us more than He can trust us with. John writes, "I wish above all things that thou mayest prosper and be in health, even as thy soul prospereth" (3 Jn. 2). We don't have to beg Him for it.

---

*T*here is no reason to be the richest man in the cemetery. You can't do any business from there.

Colonel Harlan Sanders

Finances

I believe God wants us to be good stewards of the resources that He entrusts to us. I realize that money can't buy happiness—but neither can poverty. Money is just a tool to help us meet our needs and to help us bless others. It's a gift that God gives us.

I was not educated to think and plan financially. When I was in school, the general consensus was that Jesus was coming soon, and therefore long-term financial planning was unnecessary. As a result, I got further into debt than I should have. (Of course, other factors were involved too.) Eventually I started thinking *debt-free* instead of borrowing and going further into debt. Today I believe God enough to operate on a cash basis. I think totally differently about finances from the way I used to.

Financial Goals

The Bible does not say that money is evil. It's the *love of money* that is behind a lot of evil. (See First Timothy 6:10.) Some say that money destroys people. I personally don't believe that. Money only brings out what you already are. If you are sinful with sinful ideas and you suddenly get a lot of money, you simply will be more sinful. If you are a good person, then money will bring out more of the good in you.

We need financial goals as well as plans to accomplish those goals. Debt can destroy you. Interest can eat you up. I've learned to passionately hate debt. I don't want debt to enslave me, tear me apart, destroy me, and ruin me. I believe in financial freedom for individuals, for families, for churches, and for ministries.

God isn't glorified when we are poor, sick, and broke. That is not necessarily the spiritual way we are to live. God is a great provider of all the good things in life. He will help us to understand that His blessings are our blessings. "The blessing of the Lord brings wealth, and He adds no trouble to it" (Prov. 10:22 NIV).

There is a curse of poverty on some people. God wants to break that curse and turn things around for blessing. God controls all the wealth of the world. He's got the whole world in His hands. And He wants to bless you so that you, in turn, can bless His work.

Matthew 25:14-30 tells the story of a rich man who left his property in the care of some servants while he took a long trip. Two of the servants invested their money and doubled it. The third was afraid, so he just hid his. When the man returned, he was extremely displeased with that third servant, even though he returned the original money to his master.

Gaining and using money, not hiding it or losing it, is the key to having abundance. The amazing point of this unusual passage is that everyone who has will be given more abundantly, and those who don't have much will lose what little they have. It doesn't seem right, but that's the way it is. You must be a good steward, a good business manager, with the money that God entrusts to you. You must refuse to lose and aim to gain.

Moses told the Israelites, "You may say to yourself, 'My power and the strength of my hands have produced this wealth for me.' But remember the Lord your God, for it is He who gives you the ability to produce wealth..." (Deut. 8:17-18 NIV). You can't get much plainer than that.

When Solomon built the temple for God, the value of the material he used was staggering, even by today's standards. (See First Chronicles 22.) Among the materials were one hundred thousand talents of gold. That would equal about 3,800 tons and have a value of approximately $35 billion. There also were one thousand talents of silver (about 38,000 tons), valued at over $6 billion. Add to this the iron, brass, and imported cedar, and you come up with a lot of money. God likes nice things.

I've met Christians who doubt that God wants them to get or keep a job. They say they want to be in God's will, but they feel that means they should have just enough to get by. If that is true, who will finance the work of God all over the world?

Whether or not you have money, the question is, *"Is money at the center of my attention, or is God?"* Whatever gets your attention gets you. If money is what gets your attention, then money will get you. Remember, Scripture does not say that money is evil, but "the love of money is the root of all evil" (1 Tim. 6:10a).

Satan has stolen money from a lot of people, but God has taken the wealth of the wicked and laid it up for the righteous. If you are faithful over what God has given you, Heaven will respond with material blessings in your life.

We *make a living by what we get. We make a life by what we give.*

Winston Churchill

If you want God to bless you, you can't be a tightwad. You need to be generous with the blessings God gives you. The Bible teaches tithing and giving. The increase of money into your life actually depends upon you, and upon your thinking and your believing. It depends upon your obedience to God in your

85

tithing and your giving. Your dedication to God can be seen in your checkbook.

T*he real measure of a man's worth is how much he would be worth if he lost all his money.*

Oswald J. Smith

People say, "*It's bad to have things. I don't want to be rich.*" No, it's not bad to have things; it's bad when things have you. A prosperous appearance can be an advantage in witnessing to those around you. Take Joseph. He was a man of God who prospered in what he did; he was blessed of God. He prospered over Potiphar's house; he prospered in prison. God sent blessings his way. Eventually he became second ruler in Egypt. Joseph gained, and God blessed him. Joseph continued to gather wealth for Egypt through the time of famine.

It's time for you to receive God's blessings, to gather in all that God has for you. Shampoo your mind with the Word of God. God wants you to be blessed financially. Rearrange your mental furniture about money. Start giving where it can bless others. Plant good seed in good soil.

This is so important. God is interested in more than your spiritual well-being; He is also interested in your financial well-being. Don't wait for specific instructions—financial disaster can arrive while you're still waiting to hear from God. But at the same time, don't do something foolish like borrowing money to get enough cash to make things work—creditors will only go so far. Don't rush off and sell all your assets in order to live. If you can't pay your debts on time and keep your word to your creditors, you had better take another look at things. Get some good counsel. Proverbs 13:22 says that a good man leaves an inheritance to his grandchildren.

Life Changed

A certain man, physically and mentally shattered, walked hopelessly through the halls of an asylum. At age 50, his dreams and hopes were gone, and he was nearly penniless. He owed huge debts, and he knew of no way to begin to repay them. Life itself was a burden. This broken man felt that he could not go any farther. Then he heard people singing, "Be not dismayed, whate'er betide, God will take care of you."

Suddenly the truth dawned upon him. He could hear the Lord saying, "Come unto Me, all ye that labour and are heavy laden, and I will give you rest" (Mt. 11:28). "God," he whispered, "will You help me?" Immediately defeat departed from him, and he determined that from that moment on he would serve God.

Forty-five years later, this same man—once shattered, broken, and defeated—stood at an awards banquet. He was being recognized as one of the most successful businessmen in the history of America.

He was so well known for his success that when he told this story it was hard for anyone to imagine that he had ever been on the brink of complete failure. He related his formula for success. "It was Jesus and the Scriptures," he said, that had burst into his troubled mind so many years before. At the time of this awards banquet, J.C. Penney was 95 years old. He still worked eight hours a day. He was happy, healthy, successful, and wealthy. He had rearranged his mental furniture.

The three steps to J.C. Penney's success were these: 1) come to Jesus; 2) be yoked with Him, letting Him be the boss; and 3) learn and apply His teachings. The formula worked for J.C. Penney, and it will work for you today. You may feel like you've been ripped off by the devil, but God can turn it all

87

around for you. He can give back everything that satan has destroyed for you. You can reclaim it. It is God's will.

Success can't be measured just in terms of money or fame, however. We all can have success when we trust God. It all comes down to changing our thinking. A simple saying states, "If things don't change, they will remain the same."

Recognize that satan is defeated. Any victory that he wins in your life is not because God wanted it to be that way. Satan only wins when you allow him to by the way you think and live. Don't let satan win in your life. God never intended that he should have victory over one of His children. God wants you to triumph and be victorious.

B*e an optimist, not a pessimist. I've never seen a monument erected to a pessimist.*

Paul Harvey

Stewardship

God doesn't do everything for you; He wants you to do something too. God doesn't just want you to die and go to Heaven; He wants you to live and go to work. He wants you to live for Him, to tithe and give and have your finances blessed. God is interested in you.

Accountability is a key concept in Christian stewardship. The basic job of a steward is to handle the affairs of another. All we have in this world belongs to God. "The earth is the Lord's, and the fulness thereof" (Ps. 24:1a). We will answer for how well we manage our portion of God's creation.

Dependability is another aspect of stewardship. Since we are accountable to God, we also should be dependable in honoring our promises to people and to Him, as well as in our giving.

Dependability is our response of love and gratitude to God. How much does it take to be dependable? Sure, there are minimum standards of faithfulness and dependability. The real question for each of us, though, is this: *"How much can I give back to God, who has done so much for me?"*

Availability is another key concept of stewardship. If our time is available—if we're willing to give ourselves to God—we'll make our finances available to him also.

Tithing (It's Not an Option)

When we talk about Christian giving, the term *tithing* usually comes up. Tithing is not a new concept. It predates the writing of the Old Testament, and it has been found in almost every culture of the ancient world. Giving one-tenth of our income is first mentioned in the Bible when Abraham gave a tenth of all he had to Melchizedek, a priest of the Most High God. (See Genesis 14.) Abraham's tithing pleased God, and Abraham received God's promise of increase in his life. Tithing was then incorporated into the Old Testament law, and the principle is endorsed in the New Testament.

Under the Old Testament law (see Lev. 27:30-32; Num. 18:24), the tithe was paid yearly at harvest time to support the Levitical priesthood. It consisted of one-tenth of the harvest. The plan is that we give of the firstfruits, off the top, not from what is left. Firstfruits tithing is important. (See Proverbs 3:9-10.) Although tithing is mentioned in only four places in the New Testament (see Mt. 23:23; Lk. 11:42, 18:12; Heb. 7:5-9), we know that Jesus and His first followers were Jews who would have kept the laws of tithing.

What about today's Christians and tithing? We are not legalistically bound to give a tithe, but we are morally bound to give from a heart and response of love. Since *tithe* means "one-tenth," ten percent is a good place to start. Thus our giving reveals our sincerity and our consecration to God. Giving involves our stewardship, which we've already mentioned. We give, not to buy salvation, but because of our love for God and our gratitude to Him for His blessings on our lives.

Principles for Giving

Tithing is a commandment of God; it is not an option. On the other hand, neither will it substitute for genuine Christian character. Tithing doesn't take the place of being committed to God. I don't tithe because I have to or because I have a lot. I don't wait until I can "afford to tithe." I tithe because of a deep, sincere desire to obey God.

Paul took an offering from Gentile Christians for the Jewish Christians in Jerusalem who were in need. (See Second Corinthians 8:1-15.) Paul wanted this offering to be a success. He wanted to promote unity between the factions. The Jewish Christians were somewhat hesitant about taking the gospel to the Gentiles, in spite of the charge of Jesus. They stayed around home until persecution forced them out of Jerusalem. This offering was intended to show brotherhood between Jews and Gentiles. It showed the principle of sharing, which is basic to the nature of God.

Rich industrialists like Henry Ford, John D. Rockefeller, and Andrew Carnegie built great fortunes, but their wealth did little good for others until after they died. On the other hand, Christian industrialist R.G. LeTourneau used the profits of his business to bless missions in other countries even during his lifetime. He moved his money with his heart.

People wonder why God lets them suffer when they consistently tithe. They feel that because they tithe, they shouldn't have any problems. But God allows almost everyone to be tested at times, and besides that, we live after the Fall. So tithing will not put you in a position to bargain with God.

Other people think that tithing obligates God to them, and in a certain sense that may be true. God promises to pour out a blessing on those who tithe. For some, though, this may include a blessing as they go *through* suffering.

I remember that my parents tithed. Even when members of the congregation gave them food, at least a tenth of it would be passed on to another minister. The truth is that if we can't be trusted with the money God blesses us with, we can't be trusted with anything. (I also believe that ministries should be accountable to those who bless them with finances.)

Everything belongs to God, the Chairman of our business. He has wealth beyond our imagination. So tithing also is an act of worship. When we give, we honor God's ownership of this inexhaustible wealth that He wants to use to bless us.

Every time I think of giving, I remember that God gave much more than finances. He gave His only Son. Jesus gave His life for us. The least we can do is give of our finances! Money isn't everything, and we're not working for money; we're working for God. Nevertheless, we need to give from the blessings God has given to us.

We need to give because of our gratitude to God. People give as memorials to those who have died. Maybe, instead, we should give because a loved one didn't die, because he or she was spared and protected! If you're a giver, you'll find reasons to give. If you're a tightwad, you will find reasons not to give. Everyone finds either an excuse or a reason.

Believe it or not, 100 percent of most church congregations tithe. Some give voluntarily, while God takes it from the rest one way or another. A lot of Christians act like the little boy whose mother gave him two quarters. One was for his Sunday school offering, and the other was for something that he wanted. As he walked down the street, he dropped one, and it rolled through a grate. "Well, God," he said, "I just lost Your quarter." Maybe we can learn more from the rich man whose crop wouldn't fit into his barns. He decided to build bigger barns to hold everything instead of investing God's way. As a result, those bigger barns didn't do him any good. (See Luke 12:15-21.)

Our attitude toward giving has to be right. Should we tithe to the church or somewhere else? Well, let's say I go into McDonald's and get coffee and fries but tell the cashier that I'm not going to pay for them there, I'm going to pay at Wendy's. She'll think I'm crazy. The same applies to our tithing. We should support the church where we're being fed.

Notes

1. Believe that God wants you to be a good steward of the money that comes to you.

2. Set financial goals.

3. Whatever bad financial situation you're in now, believe that God can turn it around.

Top Three Changes to Make!

1.

2.

3.

Chapter Eleven

Dating, Marriage, and Sex

Marriage is the first institution created by God. God knew that man would be lonely by himself, so He gave him a companion. She was not a clone, but a unique creation of her own. She had her own needs that only Adam could supply, just as he had needs only she could supply. "Therefore a man shall leave his father and mother and be joined to his wife, and they shall become one flesh" (Gen. 2:24 NKJV).

"And the Lord God said, It is not good that the man should be alone; I will make him an help meet for him" (Gen. 2:18). The New International Version translates *help meet* as "suitable helper."

God ordained marriage, sex, and family from the very beginning. Marriage is an institution that God has blessed. A stable marriage creates a family unit, which God intended to be the basic building block—the foundation—of society. When the family unit breaks down, all of society crumbles. We need to put Christ first in our marriage.

"And they were both naked...and were not ashamed" (Gen. 2:25). Adam and Eve shared a wonderful intimacy. They found physical fulfillment in each other. In today's society, absolute faithfulness isn't the norm. It should be. Paul wrote, "Because of immoralities, let each man have his own wife, and let each woman have her own husband" (1 Cor. 7:2 NAS).

Marriage takes work. It takes commitment. It really takes a miracle for God to bring two people together who will leave their families and become husband and wife—and succeed at it. It may be a miracle, but it's God's plan for every husband and wife to come together and make a strong marriage.

Marriage isn't so much finding the right person as being the right person.

Charlie Shedd

It makes a strong statement when two are together in a God-centered marriage. "Where two...are gathered together in My name, there am I in the midst of them" (Mt. 18:20). Marriage is a strong, holy, honorable, sacred commitment.

Dating

Sometimes young people will claim that they are dating an unsaved boy or girl in order to get them saved. However, instead of the Christian lifting up the other person, more often than not the unsaved person pulls the Christian down. The dating game is a poor mission field. Dates don't always end up in marriage, but in America, marriages are usually preceded by dating. In other words, you usually marry someone whom you have dated.

The greatest temptations come to people when they are alone and out on a date—on the beach, in a parked car, or at home when the parents are gone. If you don't think the devil is going to tempt you, you are mistaken. He will overwhelm your emotions and enflame your desires for a physical intimacy that God does not want outside of marriage. God doesn't want you to be deceived; He doesn't want you to be messed up. Satan has been in this game for a long time, and he knows how to mess you up. He plans to totally destroy you. Rearrange your mental furniture so he doesn't destroy you.

A young man in college was being teased by friends who couldn't believe that he was still a virgin. His answer was great: "Any time I want to, I can become like you, but you can never again be like me."

Over the years I have received hundreds of letters and telephone calls from young people who had become sexually active before marriage. Many tell sad stories of guilt, broken hearts, unwanted pregnancies, and sexually transmitted diseases. Their message is the same as mine: It's not worth it. You will reap what you sow. You can make excuses, ignore God, or try to run from Him, but there will come a time when the harvest appears.

The day will come when the harvest you reap will not be the one you want. With God, the harvest may not come at the end of the month, but it will come. How much better it is to keep a right relationship with God now and focus on a clean, pure life!

God can help you stay clean and pure. If you are reading this and are not married, it'll be a wonderful moment when you can say, "I totally belong to you, and only to you."

Now, don't misunderstand me. God also blesses people who remain single in life. You can be blessed either way.

When you get married, the two of you become one. You have a mind to work together, to have compassion and help one another, and to honor one another. "Husbands, dwell with them according to knowledge, giving honour unto the wife, as unto the weaker vessel, and as being heirs together of the grace of life; that your prayers be not hindered" (1 Pet. 3:7).

The Golden Rule tells us that we need to treat each other like we want to be treated. (See Matthew 7:12.) Sometimes we need to know how our spouse wants to be treated, then act that way.

Be quick to forgive, quick to honor the other person. Always take your differences to God, the One who invented marriage in the first place. Always see yourselves as one, even though you have different habits, IQ's, educational levels, backgrounds, and personalities.

Show appreciation for each other. There really is a way to solve problems without screaming at the top of your voice. We all need to learn how to control our spirits. Praying together is important. "The family that prays together stays together."

L*ord, when I am wrong, make me willing to change. When I am right, make me easy to live with. So strengthen me that the power of my example will exceed the authority of my rank.*
Pauline H. Peters

Sometimes we have to forgive and forget the past. We have to start over to make things work. It's like the coach for our baseball team. He told us that we were going to have to completely start over, because we were the worst team he had ever seen. "Sit down," he said as he held up a bat. "Now, this is a baseball bat. This is a ball. When the pitcher throws the ball, the bat is supposed to hit the ball." We started over.

Sometimes husbands cause the problems in the marriage. Other times, wives do. Rarely do big things cause the worst problems; often it's the seemingly insignificant things that happen over and over again that eventually cause a sore spot.

The only way to get the best of an argument is to avoid it.

Dale Carnegie

Some wives bother their husbands with backseat driving. They may nearly wear out the carpet on the passenger side by pushing on a brake that isn't there. Now there are even mats you can buy with a brake pedal for that kind of driver. On the other side of the coin, husbands frequently disturb their wives by ignoring them. Incredibly, there are couples who have been married more than 40 years, who then get divorced. It's often because they didn't take care of that bothersome rubbing on those little sore spots. Unfortunately, the world is constantly talking divorce. We, on the other hand, should emphasize the strength of marriage.

Fighting in our home will destroy us. We need to accept our differences, forget the little petty things, and close the door to the problems in our lives.

We must work to build or rebuild a marriage. Here's one model God offers:

1.   Humble yourself...
2.   Pray and seek God's face...
3.   Turn from your wicked ways...

Even though marriage is under attack in the world today, God will heal your marriage. (See Second Chronicles 7:14.)

Proverbs 18:22 says, "Whoso findeth a wife findeth a good thing, and obtaineth favour of the Lord."

The next two pages contain a marriage checklist. Please take a few minutes to evaluate yourself. Then have your spouse evaluate him or herself, and compare notes. Be honest. This is not a competition. It is more for information and to help both of you know and talk about what needs worked on in your marriage.

Husband's Checklist

Rate yourself on a scale of 1 to 10 (10 highest/best, 1 lowest/worst).

_____ . I married the right person.

_____ . I have been as nice to her during our marriage as I was before.

_____ . I am totally bonded to my wife and have eyes for no one else.

_____ . I really see my wife and me as one.

_____ . We have a Christian home.

_____ . I always do my best to provide what my wife needs.

_____ . I am a good sexual partner with her.

_____ . I sacrifice my own interests to do what she wants.

_____ . I tell her every day that I love and appreciate her.

_____ . I do little things she likes to please her.

_____ . I listen when she talks and show interest.

_____ . We never go to sleep angry with each other.

_____ . I don't talk about her faults to cover my own failures.

_____ . We pray daily and read God's Word together.

_____ . I sometimes control my sexual needs in order to accommodate her.

_____ . I am working on being a good husband and father.

_____ . We attend church faithfully.

Wife's Checklist

Rate yourself on a scale of 1 to 10 (10 highest/best, 1 lowest/worst).

_____ . I married the right person.

_____ . I have been as nice to him during our marriage as I was before.

_____ . I am totally bonded to my husband and have eyes for no one else.

_____ . I really see my husband and me as one.

_____ . We have a Christian home.

_____ . I always do my best to provide what my husband needs.

_____ . I am a good sexual partner with him.

_____ . I sacrifice my own interests to do what he wants.

_____ . I tell him every day that I love and appreciate him.

_____ . I do little things he likes to please him.

_____ . I listen when he talks and show interest.

_____ . We never go to sleep angry with each other.

_____ . I don't talk about his faults to cover my own failures.

_____ . We pray daily and read God's Word together.

_____ . I sometimes control my sexual needs in order to accommodate him.

_____ . I am working on being a good wife and mother.

_____ . We attend church faithfully.

Notes

1. Commit yourself to having a great marriage.

2. Put Second Chronicles 7:14 into practice in your home.

3. Make necessary changes.

Top Three Changes to Make!

(Write these after you complete and talk about the Marriage Checklist.)

1.

2.

3.

Chapter Twelve

Divine Blessing vs. Luck

Many of us, probably even most of us, have a few "pet superstitions." We don't do something a certain way because we were told as children that it was "unlucky." Or we may "knock on wood" after talking about some good thing that has happened. If someone asks us why, we probably laugh and deny that we really believe in superstition, but say that it "can't hurt." Luck, fate, and the roll of the dice are the way some people live. They have never gotten beyond those things.

I don't believe in luck, either good or bad. Things are not run by luck. I do believe in the divine blessing of God.

Suppose that a corporation was run by luck. If luck determines who does what and who goes where, every business in the world would fall apart. We can't assume that great businesses were organized on the basis of luck—that all the names were put in a hat and then drawn to decide who had what position.

It sounds stupid. Luck has nothing to do with it. Success in business is organized and planned for.

People say, "Man, it was lucky I had that idea." Thoughts, ideas, and plans are not luck. Start trusting God for all His blessings.

Take a look when someone appears to "have good luck." You'll not find any luck. You'll find someone who prepared, planned, and worked. They acquired the needed tools, education, and knowledge, and from that they achieved their success. It didn't "just happen." They learned how to manage.

---

he secret of successful managing is to keep the five guys who hate you away from the four guys who haven't made up their minds yet.
Casey Stengel

Look at someone who has had "bad luck." They had a setback. Maybe they didn't plan, prepare, or work enough. Maybe they overlooked a key factor in success. Don't waste your time thinking that you can change "luck" in your life. There is no such thing. We don't become successful through "luck." In a sense, we each decide our own future. We decide our habits, and our habits decide our future.

Success comes from doing what God wants us to do. We don't count on luck for victory in our life—nor for our marriage, for the car to run, or for winning.

When I was a child, I thought that if someone was really rich and blessed, they were probably crooked. They were dishonest. It was fate. Maybe the roll of the dice brought them to their wealth. Don't you believe it.

Divine Blessing vs. Luck

Some people think like the old man who lay in bed dying. He said to his wife, "When I limped home from the war, you were waiting for me. When I was released from Dachau at the end of the World War II, you were by my side."

Overcome with emotion he continued, "When we sold everything to start a business and it went broke and left us penniless, there you were. Now, as I breathe my last breath, here you stand by my bedside. Honey, I'm telling you, you're a jinx."

Our relationship with God, the Giver of all blessings, is the key to being divinely blessed, not luck.

When the storms of life strike, it's what happens in *you* that will determine what happens to *you*.

Jerry Savelle

Notes

1. Do not believe in luck, fate, or the roll of the dice in any manner.

2. Believe in God's divine blessings for you.

Top Three Changes to Make!

1.

2.

3.

Chapter Thirteen

The Jesus Factor

Sometimes we don't take into consideration the changes that will take place because of the *Jesus factor*. Hebrews 7:25 says, "Wherefore He is able also to save them to the uttermost that come unto God by Him, seeing He ever liveth to make intercession for them." Jesus is interceding for us, making sure we have better treatment.

Simon Peter

The *Jesus factor* allowed Peter to walk on water during a severe storm. It also saved him when he took his eyes off of Jesus. (See Matthew 14:28-33.)

Later, "the Lord said, Simon, Simon, behold, satan hath desired to have you, that he may sift you as wheat: but I have prayed for thee, *that thy faith fail not*" (Lk. 22:31-32a, emphasis added). This is the *Jesus factor*.

Disciples

Jesus' prayer in the Garden of Gethsemane asked that the will of the Father be done. His concerned prayer for His disciples in John 17 extended down through the centuries, even to us. The prayer didn't ask that we be taken out of the world, but that we be protected and kept from evil. This is the *Jesus factor*.

"At that day ye shall ask in My name: and I say not unto you, that I will pray the Father for you: for the Father Himself loveth you" (Jn. 16:26-27a).

Mother-in-Law

When Jesus saw Peter's mother-in-law lying sick in bed, He was concerned. So He healed her of a fever. (See Matthew 8:14-15.) That was the *Jesus factor*.

Family

Jesus was concerned about the grief that a family felt. He wept because of the death of Lazarus (see Jn. 11:33-36). His concern was obvious to those who were there. Here again, the *Jesus factor*.

City

"He beheld the city, and wept over it" (Lk. 19:41b). Here was the *Jesus factor* for a city.

Crowd

Five thousand were gathered on a hillside of Galilee. Jesus was concerned because He knew they must be hungry. The *Jesus factor* multiplied a child's lunch into more than enough to feed this multitude. (See John 6:1-14.)

When the *Jesus factor* takes over in your life, you can have more than enough.

Women and Servants

Examples of Jesus' concern for women, servants, and even outcasts are many: the woman with the issue of blood, Jairus' daughter, the centurion's servant, the widow of Nain, blind people, the epileptic boy. The touch of Jesus has power to heal and meet needs.

Healing

The *Jesus factor* cleansed leprosy, healed illnesses, and raised the dead. Working through Peter, the *Jesus factor* raised Dorcas from the dead. It healed the lame man at the Gate Beautiful. It also released Peter from prison.

Saul

The *Jesus factor* stopped Saul in his tracks and changed him from one of the worst persecutors of the early Church into Paul the apostle (see Acts 9). It protected the crew of the ship on the island of Melita (see Acts 27–28), and it caused an earthquake in Philippi (see Acts 16), which resulted in the conversion of the jailer.

God does not give victory over the world just to a select few. He gives an overcoming victory to every person that is born again.

Billy Joe Daugherty

For Us

Jesus is our example. "Christ also suffered for us, leaving us an example, that ye should follow His steps" (1 Pet. 2:21b).

"Whoever claims to live in Him must walk as Jesus did" (1 Jn. 2:6 NIV). He is our example. Jesus even told us that He had given us an example (see Jn. 13:12-17).

The *Jesus factor* will give us freedom. "If ye continue in My word, then are ye My disciples indeed; and ye shall know the truth, and the truth shall make you free" (Jn. 8:31b-32). Jesus is a deliverer. He gives us power. (See Luke 10:19.) He promised that nothing would hurt us. Jesus is our freedom. He is our Savior. He is our Lord.

For Others

The *Jesus factor* is love; it is concern for others. It brings us forgiveness and inner peace. The *Jesus factor* brings security. Jude 24-25 says that He is able to keep us from falling, even through eternity.

When the *Jesus factor* is working, we "can do all things through Christ" (Phil. 4:13). He'll supply all our needs (see Phil. 4:19). Whatever we need will be supplied because of the *Jesus factor*.

F*aith does not wait for walls to fall down. Faith shouts them down.*

F.F. Bosworth

The *Jesus factor* will relieve discouragement. Jesus tells us not to be discouraged (see Jn. 14:1). He tells us to give Him our worries and cares. When we do, it will take care of loneliness and uncertainty. God is our refuge.

The *Jesus factor* will allow us to work miracles. Jesus Himself said that we would do greater works than He had done, because He was going back to Heaven (see Jn. 14:12).

The Lord will take care of us even in extreme difficulty because of the *Jesus factor*. (See Second Corinthians 4:8-10.) He has promised to go with us in these times, not to keep us from them.

You also can tell when the *Jesus factor* isn't working. Anger and resentment will surface.

The difference between winning and losing for each of us is the *Jesus factor*. It will bring out the best of who we are and what we can do. It will give us authority in our life.

The real enemy of our faith is doubt (see Mt. 21:21). Doubt realizes that God's Word is true, but doesn't believe that it will work for us today. Many people are programmed to believe the worst. They find a little mole on their body, and they immediately decide that they have cancer.

Kick out doubt. Start putting faith to work and you will see the *Jesus factor* in action.

Notes

1. Believe that the *Jesus factor* can take over in your life.

2. Start thanking the Lord daily for working in your life.

Top Three Changes to Make!

1.

2.

3.

Chapter Fourteen

Changing Your Future

Jesus always kept His thoughts on His Father and His will. We can be like Him, for we have the mind of Christ. (See Philippians 2:5.)

To change our future, we must change our thinking. When a woman marries a man, she often thinks she can change him. When a man marries a woman, he thinks she will never change. Actually, both are wrong. We all change, sometimes for the better, sometimes for the worse. It all comes back, however, to the way we think. To change for the better, we need to rearrange our mental furniture.

Hijacked

Many almost-happy marriages, bright futures, conceivably successful businesses, and potentially large churches have been hijacked by thinking wrongly. We have to change our thinking if we're going to change our future. A shift in how we look at things is a necessity. The world may be constantly talking divorce, but you must build and strengthen your marriage. When businesses fall apart around you, believe that God will see you through. Believe that revival is coming to your church, and God will change an entire community. You can reach your goals when your thinking is changed, when you rearrange your mental furniture.

Romans 12:2 tells us to not be conformed to the things of this world, but to be transformed by the renewing of our mind. I hear people say that "renewing your mind" is a New Age phrase. It's not; it's a Bible phrase. New Agers are only borrowing it. It's really a "God" thing.

We can tackle any challenge. Miracles really happen when our thinking changes. Abraham changed his natural way of thinking, and he began praying for a child. (See Genesis 15:2-6.) And even though he and Sarah took things into their own hands and produced Ishmael, God answered in His time and Isaac was born. (See Genesis 21:1-3.)

If *you want to change your life, you have to change your confession.*

John Osteen

Joshua was another one who changed his natural thinking and made history. He commanded the sun and moon to stand still, and they did for the space of an entire day. (See Joshua 10:12-14.)

King Darius changed his natural thinking. When he was forced by his own decree to cast Daniel into a den of lions, he declared to Daniel, "Thy God whom thou servest continually, He will deliver thee" (Dan. 6:16b).

Elijah called up a three-and-a-half year drought. Then he called down fire from heaven. He changed the future. (See First Kings 18:17-39.)

Jesus came on the scene and changed the thinking and the future of the world. He performed miracles, healed the sick, fed multitudes, cleansed lepers, and raised the dead. He changed the natural thinking of the people to the truth that there are miracles available for them. And He said that we would do greater things than He did. (See John 14:12.)

If *you can dream it, you can do it...This whole thing was started by a mouse.*

Walt Disney

Limits

We need to take the limits off of ourselves and off of God, and change our thinking. Tell yourself, "*I can tackle any challenge.*" Paul told us in Philippians 4:8 to think on things that are true, honest, just, pure, lovely, and good. Paul faced many crises, yet he could say that God's peace kept his heart and mind. He learned how to change his future. It is by walking in a love relationship with God—depending on His power and His strength, not our own.

I tell this story often. I was working late at my office when a good friend, Woody Clark of Woodpecker Trucks, called and asked me what I was doing. I replied that I was trying to work something out. He quickly retorted, "Well, have you ever thought of having God work it out?"

I started to interrupt with, "Yes, but...."

"God can take care of it, Ken," he insisted.

I tried again, "I tried that, but...."

"God will handle it," was his response.

The next time I got a little farther. "Woody, you know I trust God, but...."

He interrupted me again. "Ken, go home, go to bed, rest in peace. Just shut up and prove that you trust God. Don't make the need bigger than God is."

I listened to Woody. I went home and got a good night's rest. And guess what—God worked the problem out.

Some people change jobs, friends, cars, homes, even mates; but they never think of changing themselves.

Jack Holt

Paul stated that "all things work together for good to them that love God" (Rom. 8:28a). He did not say that all things were good, but that if we trust God, He will make things work out and change our future for His glory.

We need to "renew our mind" so we can receive what God has for us.

Consider how hard it is to change yourself and you'll understand what little chance you have of changing others.

Jacob M. Braude

We've got to start resisting and rebuking the devil. We must have victory in our lives.

If you're a Christian, it is time you start binding satan and loosing his hold on your life. You can bind satan for years, but you also need to start loosing his hold on you—rebuking and resisting him.

Have faith and rearrange your mental furniture so your thoughts are filled with God's ways.

Faith and works should travel side by side, step after step, like the legs of men walking. First faith, then works, then faith again, then works again until you can hardly distinguish which is the one and which is the other.

William Booth

Pray this prayer:

In Jesus' Name, I come against you, satan, binding you and your past hold on my life. I block you, satan, from any future hold or effect on me, from this day forth. My life is now in God's hand, and I have the mind of Christ—His thoughts, His ways, His purposes. I rebuke and resist you, satan, and take back all you have stolen from me.

Jesus, I ask forgiveness for wrong, negative thinking. Create in me a clear heart and mind, helping me to serve You with all my heart, obeying all Your commandments. Help to keep my thoughts pleasing to You. Thank You for hearing and answering me. Amen.

Notes

1. Take limits off yourself.

2. Bind satan and loose his hold from your life now and for the future.

Top Three Changes to Make!

1.

2.

3.

Final Notes

To Help You Rearrange Your Mental Furniture

Here are some things that have helped me. I trust that they will bless your life with positive results and help you rearrange your mental furniture.

1. Begin every day with God as your partner.
2. Rebuke, resist, and reject anything that satan puts in your way.
3. Believe the fact that God is bigger than satan in your life.
4. Be a forgiving person.
5. Believe that God intends for you to solve problems, not make them.
6. Never panic when a challenge comes your way.
7. Stay cheerful, even when you're not happy. (If you get a flat tire, you're not happy, but you can still be cheerful.)
8. Control circumstances; don't let them control you.
9. Interrupt negative thoughts that come into your mind.

10. Believe that God will see you through any situation and that everything will be all right.
11. Believe that God will return many times over what satan has taken from you.
12. Attend church faithfully and win others to Christ.
13. Be a tither and a giver.
14. Fast and pray. (See Matthew 6:16-18.)
15. Obey the commandments of God.
16. Be a reader of God's Word. It is food for our spiritual lives. (A snack on Sunday morning is not enough to feed you for the whole week.)
17. Let your faith grow. Second Thessalonians 1:3 talks about our faith growing.
18. Believe God to think bigger.
19. Get involved in your church.
20. Start praising God daily—in advance—for miracles.

I do these three things daily:
1. I ask God to be with me.
2. I believe that He will answer my prayers.
3. I thank Him in advance for all that He has done for me and for what He will continue to do.

Ken Gaub travels all over the world and may be coming to your area.

If you would like to write to the author or schedule him to speak, contact him through:

Ken Gaub World Wide Ministries
Y.O.U. Productions
P.O. Box 1
Yakima, WA 98907
U.S.A.
Phone: (509) 575-1965
Fax: (509) 575-4732
email: kengaub@aol.com
website: www.kengaub.com

Exciting titles
by T.D. Jakes

— **Destiny Image proudly introduces
the T.D. Jakes Classics Gift Set**

**Includes #1 Best-Seller, *Woman, Thou Art Loosed,*
and Best-Sellers, *Can You Stand to Be Blessed,*
and *Naked and Not Ashamed***

With words that stand the test of time, T.D. Jakes' three books cross denominational lines, racial barriers, and gender biases to reach into the heart of the reader. With the compassion of Jesus Christ, he touches the hidden places of every woman's heart to bring healing to past wounds with the phenomenal best-selling *Woman, Thou Art Loosed!* With the same intensity he calls all men, women, and children to stop being afraid to reveal what God longs to heal in *Naked and Not Ashamed.* Only when we drop our masks and facades can we be real before our Lord and others. And with *Can You Stand to Be Blessed?* T.D. Jakes, a man of many accomplishments and life goals, shares personal insights that will help all people survive the peaks and valleys of daily living out God's call upon their lives. This classics gift set is sure to become a special part of every reader's personal library!
ISBN 1-56043-319-1 (Gift Set)

Also available separately.
WOMAN, THOU ART LOOSED!
ISBN 1-56043-100-8
CAN YOU STAND TO BE BLESSED?
ISBN 1-56043-801-0
NAKED AND NOT ASHAMED
ISBN 1-56043-835-5

Available at your local Christian bookstore.

**For more information and sample chapters,
visit www.reapernet.com**

6B-1:17

Books to help you grow strong in Jesus

Destiny Image titles
you will enjoy reading

Books to help you grow strong in Jesus

━ THE HIDDEN POWER OF PRAYER AND FASTING
by Mahesh Chavda.
The praying believer is the confident believer. But the fasting believer is the overcoming believer. This is the believer who changes the circumstances and the world around him. He is the one who experiences the supernatural power of the risen Lord in his everyday life. An international evangelist and the senior pastor of All Nations Church in Charlotte, North Carolina, Mahesh Chavda has seen firsthand the power of God released through a lifestyle of prayer and fasting. Here he shares from decades of personal experience and scriptural study principles and practical tips about fasting and praying. This book will inspire you to tap into God's power and change your life, your city, and your nation!
ISBN 0-7684-2017-2

━ THE LOST ART OF INTERCESSION
by Jim W. Goll.
Finally there is something that really explains what is happening to so many folk in the Body of Christ. What does it mean to carry the burden of the Lord? Where is it in Scripture and in history? Why do I feel as though God is groaning within me? No, you are not crazy; God is restoring genuine intercessory prayer in the hearts of those who are open to respond to His burden and His passion.
ISBN 1-56043-697-2

━ ENCOUNTERING THE PRESENCE
by Colin Urquhart.
What is it about Jesus that, when we encounter Him, we are changed? When we encounter the Presence, we encounter the Truth, because Jesus is the Truth. Here Colin Urquhart, best-selling author and pastor in Sussex, England, explains how the Truth changes facts. Do you desire to become more like Jesus? The Truth will set you free!
ISBN 0-7684-2018-0

━ WORSHIP: THE PATTERN OF THINGS IN HEAVEN
by Joseph L. Garlington.
Worship and praise play a crucial role in the local church. Whether you are a pastor, worship leader, musician, or lay person, you'll find rich and anointed teaching from the Scriptures about worship! Joseph L. Garlington, Sr., a pastor, worship leader, and recording artist in his own right, shows how *worship is the pattern of things in Heaven*!
ISBN 1-56043-195-4

━ RELEASERS OF LIFE
by Mary Audrey Raycroft.
Inside you is a river that is waiting to be tapped—the river of the Holy Spirit and power! Let Mary Audrey Raycroft, a gifted exhorter and teacher and the Pastor of Equipping Ministries and Women in Ministry at the Toronto Airport Christian Fellowship, teach you how you can release the unique gifts and anointings that the Lord has placed within you. Discover how you can move and minister in God's freeing power and be a releaser of life!
ISBN 1-56043-198-9

Available at your local Christian bookstore.

For more information and sample chapters, visit www.reapernet.com

6B-1:12